How Stella Saved the Farm

A Tale About Making Innovation Happen

Vijay Govindarajan and Chris Trimble
Illustrations by Keny Widjaja

'This elegant story, rich in insight into what it takes to make innovation happen, has already had tremendous impact in GE executive development programmes and on key innovation projects'
Stephen Liguori, Executive Director of Global Innovation
and New Models, General Electric

'Govindarajan and Trimble have managed to do the unthinkable: develop a case study that is both seriously thought-provoking and truly entertaining'   Dolph Johnson,
Senior Vice President of Human Resources, Hasbro

'Simple. Powerful. Memorable. This story resonates with our own experiences'   Jonathan Hornby, Director of Worldwide Marketing,
SAS Institute, and author of *Radical Action for Radical Times*

A note on the authors

Vijay Govindarajan is the Earl C. Daum 1924 Professor of International Business and founding director of the Tuck School's Center for Global Leadership. He has worked with dozens of Fortune 500 corporations and speaks at conferences around the world. He lives in New Hampshire.

Chris Trimble has dedicated more than ten years to studying a single challenge that vexes even the best-managed corporations: how to execute an innovation initiative. With Govindarajan he co-authored the *New York Times* bestseller *Reverse Innovation*. He lives in Vermont.

For more information,
please visit www.howstellasavedthefarm.com

First published 2012 in the USA by St Martin's Press

First published in Great Britian 2013 by Macmillan
an imprint of Pan Macmillan, a division of Macmillan Publishers Limited
Pan Macmillan, 20 New Wharf Road, London N1 9RR
Basingstoke and Oxford
Associated companies throughout the world
www.panmacmillan.com

ISBN 978-0-230-76136-0 HB
ISBN 978-0-230-76429-3 TPB

1 3 5 7 9 8 6 4 2

A CIP catalogue record for this book is available from
the British Library.

Printed and bound in India by Replika Press Pvt. Ltd.

Visit **www.panmacmillan.com** to read more about all our books
and to buy them. You will also find features, author interviews and
news of any author events, and you can sign up for e-newsletters
so that you're always first to hear about our new releases.

Preface

The power of the fable as a teaching tool has been proven throughout the ages. If you grew up in the Western world, for example, you probably remember well the childhood lessons of Aesop's fables, such as *The Tortoise and the Hare* and *The Boy Who Cried Wolf.*

Fables can be as powerful for adults as they are for young people. In fact, two such fables helped inspire this book. George Orwell's classic, *Animal Farm,* illuminated the hidden dangers of communism. And, John Kotter's fable, *Our Iceberg Is Melting,* embedded principles for change management within a delightful tale about a colony of penguins.

We have used *How Stella Saved the Farm* with audiences ranging from senior executives to frontline employees to graduate students. We have seen that storytelling works. It catalyzes the learning process. It cuts through complexities and details, and it invites lively, insightful discussion. We have found that we are able to cover more ground in three hours with an audience that has read *Stella* than in a full day with an audience that has not.

How Stella Saved the Farm is grounded in over a decade of research. The story is a composite of dozens of innovation initiatives we have observed in established organizations. In pilot programs with early readers, several participants told us they thought the book must have been based on their own companies. That's how we knew *Stella* was doing its job.

Our intent in this book is to focus on a handful of the most fundamental principles for managing an innovation initiative, not to thoroughly examine the subject. For readers looking for a more complete and traditional treatment, we suggest *The Other Side of Innovation: Solving the Execution Challenge* (Harvard Business Review Press, 2010). That book is based on the same research as this book, but it offers in-depth recommendations, comprehensive analysis, and numerous real-world examples of innovation inside recognizable companies like IBM, BMW, and Deere & Company.

But, honestly, you'll get more out of *The Other Side* if you read *Stella* first. You'll just need to be able to withstand the fun of a narrative that is lighthearted in tone despite its serious intent.

To get the most out of *Stella,* be sure to save some time for the Study Guide, which includes Questions for Review, Questions for Deeper Reflection, and, most importantly, Lessons to Remember. Also, readers whose first language is not English and are not familiar with the vocabulary of farming may appreciate the glossary at the back of the book.

Prologue

The airline announced the final boarding call and Stella gave Alejandro one last hug. She leaned into his strong body and nuzzled his long neck. Finally, she turned and walked toward the gate. *How had this happened?* Stella had hoped to fall in love someday, but she hardly expected it to happen so soon.

Stella had high aspirations, and she didn't regard getting swept off her feet as an aspiration at all. Only a few months earlier, she had graduated from school with the firm expectation that she would change the world. Of course, she wasn't sure exactly *how* she would change the world, but she was eager to get going—working for her family's substantial farming operation, gaining real-world experience, and building skills for the future.

Stella's mother, hardly a Type A like Stella, had offered some parental advice. "You have the rest of your life to work," she told her daughter. "And work's not all it's cracked up to be. See the world first. Enjoy yourself."

So Stella had postponed her career plans. She had purchased a backpack, a discount airline ticket, and a guidebook, *Peru on Ten Dollars Per Day*. She was prepared to rough it, with one exception. There was no way she would let go of her BlackBerry.

She started her trip in the mountains, hiking the Inca Trail. She made friends with other backpackers from around the world, intoxicated by their unusual backgrounds, interests, and perspectives. One day, she made the difficult ascent to Machu Picchu, the famous Inca ruin. A thick mist had settled over the summit. Stella took a break, resting on a rock.

That's when Alejandro appeared through the fog.

"Care for a cherry Life Saver?" he offered.

Stella looked up—*way up*—to make eye contact. Alejandro was tall. He was handsome. Like the country of Peru itself, he seemed so, so . . . *exotic.*

"Sure. Have a seat," she invited.

For the next few months, they traveled together— Stella discovering a foreign world, Alejandro exploring his own country, each learning about the other. They photographed strange birds in the Amazon. They sunned themselves on beaches. They braved the catacombs beneath a centuries-old monastery in Lima.

Stella couldn't deny her physical attraction to Alejandro. She admired his rugged, fit form. Yet he also conveyed an air of luxuriousness, even softness. Stella found the combination irresistible.

Now, after her whirlwind romance, Stella walked onto the plane in deep thought. Leaving Alejandro was not her only source of anxiety. She checked her Black-Berry again. More bad news from Deirdre, her mentor at Windsor Farm. The economics of the farming operation were steadily deteriorating. Deirdre was under extraordinary pressure.

It was time, Stella knew, to head home and try to help. She squirmed in her seat, unable to get comfortable. Airplane seats just weren't designed for bodies like hers.

You see, Stella was a sheep.

Alejandro was an alpaca.

And this, indeed, is a fable.

Will Stella save the farm?

(The title of the book says she does, doesn't necessarily make it so!)

Part 1

Chapter 1

Three Months Earlier . . .

DEIRDRE SETTLED IN behind her large mahogany desk, custom made for a horse. Two new e-mails appeared on her computer screen. She first read the one from her broker, reminding her to lock in a price for fall corn. She made a mental note of it. Deirdre had been managing Windsor Farm's corn and soybean crops for about a year, and she enjoyed the challenge.

The other e-mail, from her young protégé Stella, described the magic of the Inca Trail. Stella wrote so descriptively about her adventures that Deirdre could almost imagine herself in Peru. Still, Deirdre thought, it would be nice to have Stella back at Windsor. She was the most unsheepish sheep Deirdre had ever encountered, a born leader.

Hooves sounded outside her office. Deirdre's father, Marcus, filled the doorframe. He looked powerful as always, though unusually tired. Marcus had run the farm for over two decades, modernizing the operation and nearly quadrupling its size. Experienced, knowledgeable, and wise, he was respected both on and off the farm.

"How are my grandsons?" Marcus began with his usual greeting. "Keeping up with their studies?"

Deirdre smiled, thinking about her energetic colts, Russell and Thomas. "They're keeping up just fine," she answered. "I'm the one who has trouble keeping up with them."

But Marcus obviously had something else on his mind. "Deirdre, there comes a time in every stallion's life when it becomes necessary to confront retirement. I've come to that point. I am ready."

What? Of course, everyone on the farm knew Marcus would have to retire at some point, but it was an eventuality Deirdre preferred to keep at a distance.

"Dad, of course, I—everyone in our farm family—will support your choice. You've certainly earned a nice retirement. But why now? You seem as on top of your game as ever."

Marcus ran a remarkably tight and efficient business. He inspired operational excellence throughout the farm. Deirdre smiled, thinking about how Windsor's managers were almost obsessed with finding opportunities to improve performance.

"I'm not doing the farm any favors by continuing as its leader," said Marcus. "I've done what I can. I have but one more responsibility: to make sure the farm is in good hands for the future."

"Dad, have you told Bull yet?" Deirdre could just picture enormous Bull bucking for joy at the news. Bull was Windsor's second-in-command. He headed bovine ops, the farm's dairy business, and ran it like a finely tuned milking machine. He was strong, dominant, and so bull-headed that everyone used his obvious nickname, Bull, rather than his given name, Harold.

"Deirdre, we need to talk," Marcus lowered his voice. "I no longer believe Bull is the right choice to succeed me."

Deirdre was stunned. "But Bull has been your number two for years—always right by your side!"

"That's exactly the problem. Bull will run the business exactly as I do. That's not what this farm needs. Every day it becomes more obvious that efficiency is no longer enough—at least, if we want to keep this a family-run company."

Deirdre needed a moment to think. She glanced out her window to the pastures beyond. The day was spectacularly sunny. The sheep grazed peacefully in the distance.

Decades ago, when animals had first started running their own farms, they had quickly demonstrated an intuitive grasp of agriculture. Humans, however, had been quicker to put machines to work. Marcus had taken a few steps in that direction, acquiring two prized tractors he kept in top shape. (He sometimes referred to the tractors as the *real* workhorses at Windsor, though that remark hadn't gone over too well with some of the touchier team members.) Could things really be as bad as her father was suggesting?

Marcus interrupted Deirdre's musings. "Human-run farms just keep consolidating and using ever more sophisticated machines. You know their motto: *Bigger is cheaper.* If we don't do something soon, the notion of an animal-run farm could become as outdated as the horse-drawn plow."

Deirdre had never seen her father so agitated.

"Our farm has grown," Marcus continued, "but it is still small by comparison. We can try to play the size game, but *family first* has always been our most cherished principle."

"As it should be, Dad," agreed his daughter.

Marcus looked spent, his forelock uncharacteristically disheveled beneath his hat. "I'm going to tell you something in complete confidence, Deirdre. I keep getting calls from people who want to buy our farm. McGillicuddy has mentioned the possibility at least three times."

Deirdre felt the hair along her braided mane stand up. The competition between animal-run and human-run farms was ever present. For the most part, it was a rivalry of mutual respect. But McGillicuddy, a human who ran the giant operation adjacent to Windsor Farm, had never accepted the modern reality of animals running their own farms. He also was notorious for his poor treatment of working animals.

"I'm worried," Marcus said. "Someday, we may have no choice but to sell. It's happened to some of our friends."

"But you run a much better farm. . . ."

"It could happen to us!" Marcus cut off his daughter's protest. This was no time to sugarcoat the situation. "We need a new kind of leader. Someone creative. Someone courageous. Someone capable of taking the farm in new directions." He looked his daughter in the eye. "Ever since you were young, you've shown that you have a different kind of mind. You have always been one to see beyond the obvious, to spot the unusual solution."

Deirdre swallowed hard. Was this going where she thought it was?

"I want you to take on the responsibility of running the farm," Marcus said.

Deirdre thought of the small team she currently managed—how far they had come, how proud she was of them. But was she ready to take responsibility for overseeing the entire farm?

"Dad, I've just started running my own division. The job of leading the farm calls for someone more experienced, more ambitious. . . ."

"Deirdre, you're Windsor's best hope for enduring success. And let me make one thing very clear. I'm not giving you the job because you are my daughter. You almost certainly would have run the farm after Bull anyway. I'm giving you the job because you are the right horse at the right time."

Deirdre studied her favorite photograph of Russell and Thomas, with Russell looking straight at the camera with a big horsey grin and Thomas engaged in watching something just off camera.

Was their future on Windsor Farm really in jeopardy?

Next to the photo of her boys was one of her late mother, who had always told her she was destined to do great things. Beside that was a picture of her beloved late husband, who had been killed in a tractor accident just one week after she had given birth to the colts.

"So, will you accept the job?"

Deirdre met her father's tired, kind gaze. She thought about how much time and energy he had devoted to helping her raise Russell and Thomas. She knew there was one thing she could not do, one word she could not utter.

She couldn't possibly say *no*.

Will Marcus save the farm?

Will Deirdre save the farm?

Chapter 2

MARCUS SPENT THE following week meeting discreetly with Deirdre to help her prepare to take over. Now it was time to break the news to Bull.

Marcus called Deirdre and Bull into his office. As he walked in, Bull noticed the portrait of Marcus hanging on the wall. Someday, he thought, it will be *my* portrait in that spot.

After exchanging pleasantries, Marcus explained quickly and directly what was about to happen. Bull sat in stunned silence for a moment, then lowered his head and charged out of the office.

"Let him run off some steam," Marcus said to Deirdre.

An hour later, Deirdre found Bull in the sheep pasture bristling, shaking his head angrily, and pawing the ground with his forehooves, sending the dirt flying behind him. His ill temper frightened the sheep, and their frantic bleats filled the air. Some had managed to climb into a tree. One poor ewe was hanging from a branch, scared to death even though she was, at most, two feet off the ground.

Bull caught sight of Deirdre and snorted. Deirdre approached him cautiously and invited him to sit beside her in the shade. She knew that somehow she needed to win him over.

Reluctantly, Bull trotted over, all 2,800 pounds of him. All the sheep, except the one dangling from the tree, took the opportunity to run for the hills.

"You were expecting to be the next leader of the farm," said Deirdre gently.

"*Everyone* was expecting I would be next."

"Including me," said Deirdre. "Can I ask what were your plans for the farm?"

"You know my motto: *Faster. Stronger. More efficient.*" Bull had posted it over his desk. "We're a well-run farm, but we could be better," he said. "I have lots of ideas for improvement. I'm ready for more responsibility."

"You are indeed, Bull. You are indeed."

Bull sighed. "I love this farm, Deirdre. But there are other farms that need good leadership."

Deirdre had anticipated this response. She knew the depth of Bull's pride. "*This* farm needs your leadership."

"This farm has *your* leadership," he countered.

"Bull, think for just a moment what would happen in your absence. You know every aspect of this farm like the back of your hoof. The other animals look up to you! Well," Deirdre nudged him, "at least when they're not afraid of you."

Bull managed a smile at the ribbing.

The two sat for a while without speaking, taking in the pastoral beauty around them—the rolling hills, the big red barn, the freshly painted farmhouse in the distance. Everything was perfectly maintained.

They watched as Maisie, a pretty little Holstein, strolled toward them. She was the farm's top milk producer at eleven gallons a day, but what she was really known for was her passion for fashion. In fact, the only mirror on the entire farm was in Maisie's pink stall. Today, she was wearing one of many hats from her rather large collection.

"Do you like my new chapeau?" Maisie tilted her head just so.

"I *do* like your hat," Bull replied, hoping Maisie would move along.

Deirdre could see that Maisie felt even more excited about her hat than usual, but it wasn't obvious to her why this one was special. The hat *did* look elegant, but it wasn't as over-the-top as many of Maisie's fashion selections.

"It's very pretty. What do you like best about it?" Deirdre asked.

"It's made of the softest wool I've ever felt," said Maisie, holding out the hat to Deirdre and Bull so they could experience its luxurious feel. "It's *imported*!" Maisie bragged. "Stella sent it to me from Pee-Roo!"

As soon as Maisie was out of earshot, Bull and Deirdre started laughing—deep, tension-releasing belly laughs. After they regained their composure, Deirdre spoke first.

"I need you, Bull."

Bull cocked his head. "You need me to do what?"

"I'm creating a new position for you: chief operating officer of the farm."

Bull smiled, flattered. It sounded like a very important job. But then it dawned on him that this job, however important, was not the same as leading the farm. It was not his dream. And it meant working for Deirdre, who was a lot younger than he was!

Sensing his thoughts, Deirdre said, "Please just think about it."

Later that day, when she returned to the sheep pasture, Deirdre saw that Bull was back to glowering, flinging dirt, and scaring the sheep.

Will Bull save the farm?

Will Maisie save the farm?

Chapter 3

DEIRDRE SURVEYED THE long, narrow rows of soybeans in the well-tended field before her. The seeds were maturing nicely. The sight calmed her frayed nerves. Two weeks after taking over management of the farm, she knew most of the animals were still not convinced of her leadership capabilities. And she was exhausted! She had never truly understood how hard Marcus worked.

A young stallion galloped toward her. Even from a distance she could tell it was Mav. Deirdre admired the perfection of his gait. Mav had been the quarterback of his high school football team (equine division), where he had earned the nickname "Maverick" because of his tendency to think he knew more than the coach. Deirdre appreciated Mav's confidence, talent, and energy, if not his unbridled ambition.

"Deirdre, come quick." Mav stopped so short he reared up on his hind legs. "Your father is very sick!"

Deirdre tried her best to keep up with Mav as they galloped the hilly half mile to the farmhouse. When she arrived at her father's bedside, Marcus clearly appeared unwell. He was sweating profusely and his breathing was noisy and labored. Worse yet, he was sleeping in an odd position. The news from the doctor was grim. Now Deirdre understood her father's decision to turn over the reins early. He must have known he was ailing.

Deirdre spent as much time with Marcus as she could over the next few weeks. Meanwhile, the farm leaders voted unanimously to award Marcus the Medal of Merit, the farm's rarest and highest honor. At the ceremony, Russell and Thomas draped the medal around their grandfather's neck while all the gathered animals—cows, sheep, roosters, chickens, turkeys, and horses—gave Marcus a deafening ovation.

"Thank you," Marcus replied hoarsely.

The next day, with Deirdre by his side, Marcus died peacefully in his sleep.

🐎 🐎 🐎

"Tell us a story," Thomas and Russell pleaded to their mother as they got into their beds. Ever since the colts had become voracious readers themselves, they rarely asked Deirdre to read aloud. But in the days following their grandfather's death, they needed their mother more than ever.

Deirdre decided it was the perfect occasion to retell the story of Windsor Farm.

"Once upon a time, there was a small farm run by a human family called the Windsors," she began. "The Windsors loved one animal in particular—John Patrick, whom everyone called JP. He was Marcus's grandfather and your great-great-grandfather."

"And JP was the smartest horse anyone had ever seen!" Russell chimed in.

Deirdre smiled. The boys had heard this story many times before. "But the Windsors didn't know the half of it," she continued. "JP taught himself to read. As far as we know, he was the first horse to do so.

"JP fervently believed that animals deserved better lives." Deirdre paused to smooth down Thomas's forelock. "Horses in particular were expected to do all the hard work, and reaped few of the benefits."

"No fair!" both boys shouted in unison.

"Right," Deirdre nodded. "So, slowly but surely, JP taught his fellow animals to read."

"Then, one day, the Windsors, who had grown old, just abandoned the farm. JP knew instantly what he wanted to do. He convinced the animals they could run the farm on their own. The very next day, JP's son Frederick, your great-grandfather, painted a new sign and hung it by the front gate. It read, WINDSOR FARM. PROUDLY RUN BY THE ANIMALS."

Russell and Thomas rested back on their pillows, knowing the story was almost over.

"Soon, JP was running the best farm in six counties. He worked hard in the field during the day and studied the books in the Windsor family library at night. Meanwhile, the news about Windsor spread. Before long, you could find farms proudly run by animals in every town. And it soon became clear—"

"—That animals are the better farmers!" cried all three in unison.

"After JP retired," Deirdre said, "young Frederick, like his father, became a great leader. He created the Animal Rights Movement that has improved all our lives."

"But by the time your grandfather took over Windsor Farm, times were changing," she said softly. "The animals were more skilled at farming, but people were more adept with machines. As they built better tractors and implements, the human-run farms became more efficient."

Deirdre gently kissed both of her now sleeping sons on the tops of their heads.

"*Bigger is cheaper,*" she finished in a whisper, recalling her father's words.

Deirdre went to her own bed and closed her eyes, but she doubted she'd sleep.

Will Mav save the farm?

Chapter 4

"*C*OCK-A-DOODLE-DOO!*"

Deirdre jolted awake. The ear-piercing call had come from Einstein, a rooster and the farm's quirky head of research. Long ago, Einstein had discovered a combination of seed and fertilizer that increased crop yields by 50 percent. Since then, he'd been given the freedom to spend his time as he wished, which meant he spent almost every waking minute in his laboratory.

Despite the fact that Einstein thought he was far too valuable for menial tasks, he jealously guarded the job of waking up everyone in the morning. He did it with exuberance, jumping up and down and flapping his wings as he let loose his high-decibel call to action.

Deirdre contemplated the day ahead. No doubt it would be much like the previous one. Since Marcus's death almost a month earlier, the animals were just going through the motions. The crops were tended, the cows were milked, and the sheep shorn and their wool taken to market, but the animals' spirits were low. Bull was as unhappy as ever. In fact, he seemed to have turned scaring sheep into a form of therapy.

After breakfast, the Count, the farm's accountant and its only turkey, handed Deirdre a monthly income statement. "It's nothing to crow about," he warned. The Count had no fewer than four pencils stuck beneath his wing. You could count on the Count to count every penny.

Deirdre surveyed the statement, which showed the performance of the farm's three major business units: ovine ops, bovine ops, and crops. (Windsor also sold some eggs, but the handful of chickens still on the farm were there mostly for sentimental reasons.)

Overall, Deirdre determined, the farm was operating as efficiently as ever. That was the good news. But prices for the farm's products were dropping across the board, squeezing profits. If current trends continued, Windsor could be forced out of business in just a few years.

Deirdre tracked down Bull in the dining stall, munching on some sweet hay. Thankfully, he was in a relatively calm mood. She told him about the reports.

Bull considered the situation and then said simply, "I will work harder."

The rest of the day Deirdre spent talking with other team leaders, looking for ideas and inspiration. At lunchtime, she sat with three almost inseparable friends: Rambo, a ram who ran ovine ops; Rex, a bull who assisted Bull in bovine ops; and Rob, the horse who had replaced Deirdre as head of crops management. Bull was a mentor to each of them, earning such loyalty that the other animals referred to the trio as the Three Little Bulls.

"How would *you* improve the farm's finances?"

Deirdre asked each of them.

Rambo (his given name was Bo, but he much preferred Rambo) described a plan to increase yarn-making capacity through better scheduling.

Rex talked about new feed for the cows that promised to increase milk production.

Rob shared news, which he had just learned, of a more effective crop rotation method.

These were good ideas, Deirdre knew, but they wouldn't be enough. She needed something far more radical.

The next few weeks, things actually got worse, not better. A hailstorm damaged the barn. A mysterious swarm of insects attacked the corn. And one night, a group of sheep managed to wander off the property and get lost.

"Why was the back gate left open?" Deirdre demanded.

Rambo told her it had been Marcus's habit to walk around the perimeter of the farm every evening, making sure all the gates were closed. Deirdre sighed and added it to her mental *to-do* list.

The next evening at sunset, Deirdre made the rounds to check the gates. She found the exercise soothing. It gave her time to think. No wonder Marcus had made it a habit.

As she walked along the rural highway at the back of the farm, her peace was interrupted by an obnoxious rumble. She turned, expecting to see an 18-wheeler. Instead, what she saw made her jaw drop.

It was a gigantic red tractor. Deirdre pulled out her cell phone and snapped a picture. When the tractor rolled to a stop next to her, she recognized the driver as McGillicuddy. His slow, deliberate descent down the ladder made the tractor seem even bigger.

"Nice evening," he said. He tipped his seed cap and hooked his thumbs in the side pockets of his overalls.

Deirdre nodded.

"Sorry to hear about Marcus."

"Thank you," said Deirdre.

"How's business?"

"The market's tough, but we're doing great."

"Market's tough, alright." McGillicuddy squinted, obviously sizing her up. Finally, he spoke. "You're a horse of few words . . . just like your father."

Deirdre nodded.

McGillicuddy scratched his bald head, replaced the seed cap, and slowly climbed up the tractor's ladder.

Later that night, Deirdre awoke in a cold sweat. In her nightmare, McGillicuddy had captured her, tied her up, climbed on his enormous tractor, and *slowly ran her over*. Then he shifted the monster machine into reverse . . . and ran over her again!

Will Einstein save the farm?

Will Rambo save the farm?

Chapter 5

WE NEED A NEW *kind of leader. Someone creative. Some-one courageous. Someone capable of taking the farm in new directions."* For the next few weeks, Marcus's words echoed ceaselessly in Deirdre's head. She wasn't clear exactly what her father had expected her to do, but she knew the time had come for her to do something.

She decided to call a farm-wide meeting. As was tradition, all the animals gathered in the large grassy area by the barn. The horses and cows sat in the grass, while the sheep climbed atop hay bales to make themselves appear taller.

Deirdre stood in front of the gathering, next to a flip chart. She began by thanking everyone for their hard work during a difficult time. "We all miss Marcus," she said, "but we must put the past behind us. As of today, all of us must shift our focus to the future. And I'm not talking about our work schedules for tomorrow or next week or next month. I'm talking about the future of the farm itself.

"First, the good news." She flipped to a simple graph

that depicted a steady decline in the farm's costs per unit production. She went on to list the many initiatives the farm had implemented over the years to achieve its tremendous efficiency.

"Everybody, let's congratulate ourselves for our enviable efficiency!"

The sheep bleated, the horses neighed, the cows mooed, the chickens clucked. Einstein crowed. Mav impressed everyone by dancing on two legs. Bull swaggered. Only the Count remained dour.

Deirdre motioned for the animals to settle down. "Now, for the bad news." She flipped the chart to another graph illustrating both the decline in the farm's costs and the even more rapid decline of the *prices* the farm received in the market. She pointed to the latter. The managers in the crowd nodded. Deirdre had already shown them the chart. Now, she knew, she needed to galvanize the working animals.

"The gap between price and cost represents the farm's income and therefore our standard of living. As it shrinks, so does our well-being."

She noticed to her exasperation that Maisie and a few others were giggling about something. As always, the working animals had little patience for numbers talk. Deirdre decided to improvise.

"Everyone, listen! Two nights ago, I had a horrible dream!"

Maisie came to attention. So did some straying sheep. Everyone loved a good story.

"And in that nightmare," Deirdre continued, "I was *run over* by *THIS!*"

On a white sheet she'd hung on the side of the barn,

Deirdre projected the photo she had taken of her neighbor's gigantic red tractor. There was collective *ooohing* and *aaahing* from the animals.

"This is McGillicuddy's new tractor," Deirdre explained. "The rear tires alone are taller than me. And human farmers are buying *thousands* of these machines. Do you know what this means?"

One of the young rams cried out excitedly, "We're going to buy one! Can I be the first to drive it? Please?"

That was not the reaction Deirdre was looking for. "This monster of a tractor would only make sense for a farm ten times the size of ours," she explained.

She went on to tell her captivated audience that even though Windsor Farm had become much bigger under Marcus's leadership, it still wasn't keeping up with the rate at which human farms were consolidating.

"My friends, we are on a slow path to oblivion. Three years from now, maybe four or five at most, we will have no choice but to *sell* Windsor Farm. And McGillicuddy is chomping at the bit to buy us out!"

The animals started yelling. Selling the farm—*especially to McGillicuddy*—was unthinkable.

Deirdre called for quiet. Every pair of eyeballs was watching her. "Yes. That's how I feel about it, too," she continued. "I've spoken with several of you about how we can improve the farm and I've heard some interesting ideas. But let me be clear. None of these ideas are *bold* enough. They will do no more than make us *slightly more efficient.*"

She paused to let the message sink in and then made her appeal. "What we need, my friends, are *great ideas for entirely new businesses.*"

Bull snorted. Rambo, Rex, and Rob, all standing next to Bull, looked perplexed. Deirdre knew she couldn't falter now. She thought of her father's words: "We need a new kind of leader. Someone creative. Someone courageous. Someone capable of taking the farm in new directions."

She pulled down several horse blankets that were hanging on the barn. Beneath in fresh paint was a notice that read

A FARMTASTIC CONTEST
IT'S A **BIG IDEA HUNT**
FOR THE FUTURE OF THE FARM
ALL ANIMALS WELCOME!

Deirdre filled in everybody on what they needed to know for the contest. For the past three weeks, she had

been gathering information from customers, analyzing markets, and projecting trends in the business environment.

"So, are you ready to come up with some Big Ideas?" she asked the crowd.

"Ready!" the animals hollered. To most of them, the contest sounded like fun.

"We'll meet back here in two weeks to choose the very best farmtastic ideas!"

Later that night, Bull and the Three Little Bulls were playing poker in a back stall of the barn.

"Why is she talking about new businesses?" Rambo grumbled. "We're farmers!"

"This is no time to take a big gamble." Rex threw a bunch of chips onto the center of the table, upping the ante. "We should focus on improving the business we have," he said.

"No kidding. We *definitely* don't need distractions right now," Rob agreed, munching on a few sugar cubes.

"Gentlemen," Bull interjected, "your concerns are reasonable. But let's support Deirdre—for now. She'll figure out soon enough that this is not the time to be chasing new ideas."

The Three Little Bulls snorted and went back to their game.

Chapter 6

TWO WEEKS LATER, all the animals gathered eagerly by the barn. Nearly forty small groups were prepared to present new ideas.

"Each team has five minutes to present," Deirdre told them. She could feel the creative energy within the crowd. She motioned for the first group to come forward.

Just then, a rusty pickup truck came into view, chugging down the farm's long dirt lane. The vehicle stopped by the barn. To everyone's delight, out jumped Stella!

Deirdre hugged her and quickly explained the contest. Stella set down her backpack and sat on a hay bale. What perfect timing, she thought, as the first group, a flock of sheep, stepped forward to present.

Their idea was a new business selling ice cream made from ewes' milk.

Next, a team of young stallions suggested a racetrack near the highway.

Maisie proposed creating a magazine, *Bovine Style,* featuring the latest trends in luxury fashion. She had

even mocked up a cover showing a Holstein in a frilly purple dress. Stella was pleased to see her friend was wearing the hat she had sent from Peru. Now *that's* luxury fashion, Stella thought.

Luxury fashion. Stella had a flash of inspiration. But was it worth sharing?

Through the parade of presentations, Deirdre was pleased with the animals' enthusiasm. The creativity! The earnestness! *The future of the farm!*

Einstein was the final presenter. He squawked about a plan to produce enormous eggs from genetically enhanced chickens. Ever the mad scientist, he drew formulas and equations on the barn wall with chalk.

As Einstein finished, Stella felt a wave of tension wash over her. Should she or shouldn't she? All the other presenters were well prepared, but she'd had no time at all to think through her idea.

"Thank you, Einstein," Deirdre said, gently escorting the flapping rooster off the presentation platform. "And thank you, everyone, for your ingenuity."

"Excuse me," said Stella, her heart racing, "but I'd like to present an idea, too."

Deirdre smiled at her protégé. Why wasn't she surprised? She invited Stella to come forward.

"My idea," Stella explained, "is that Windsor Farm should sell the *highest quality wool in the world.*"

Silence. The sheep looked particularly perplexed. A few started whispering among themselves.

Rambo stepped forward. "Ah, Stella, are you forgetting? Our wool is *already* of very high quality."

"Oh yes, of course, Rambo. There's no question about that."

"Then what exactly is your *new* idea?" Rambo asked.

"Let me explain. You see—" Stella paused, then grabbed her backpack and withdrew a poster. She tacked it on the wall, obscuring one of Einstein's formulas. The crowd pushed forward to get a closer look.

"What the heck *is* it?" a sheep called out.

"This is a picture of my friend Alejandro. I met him in Peru." Stella's tone made it obvious she had a special affection for this "friend."

"What happened to his neck?" asked a cow.

"Alejandro is an *alpaca*," Stella explained.

"A pack of what?" asked one of the chickens.

"He looks like a furry little camel," squawked another.

"Yes! He appears to be of the *camelid* family," Einstein noted, scratching his crest.

"That's right, Einstein," said Stella. "Alpaca actually have quite a bit in common with camels, except they are native to South America. You could also think of an alpaca as a very rugged sheep with a long neck," she explained. "And here is the best part: alpaca wool is incredibly soft."

"Stella's right!" Maisie removed her hat and twirled it around. "Alpaca wool is so soft! It's out of this world!"

Stella reached into her backpack again and pulled out a scarf, her going-away present from Alejandro. She invited the animals to feel for themselves. They all *ooohed* and *aaahed*.

"It wouldn't be that hard for us to produce this," Stella continued, "because alpaca care is not that different from sheep care, and we are already good at making yarn. It's just a matter of bringing in alpaca from Peru . . . and making *the world's finest yarn*." Stella noticed some of the sheep looked especially long-faced at this last remark. "The world's finest *alpaca* yarn," she qualified.

Two hours later, Deirdre reassembled the animals. "Bull and I have chosen the top finalists of the Farmtastic Contest!" she announced. Bull nodded but didn't look entirely happy. "At this point, the process gets much more serious. Each team will have to write a thorough business plan to prove their idea is solid."

Pausing briefly to heighten the suspense, Deirdre then announced the finalists. A team of older horses would work on a plan for a tourist attraction and historical site to commemorate the first animal-run farms. Three chickens would develop their idea for a new chain of local restaurants specializing in eggs, eggs, and more eggs (all farm fresh from Windsor, of course). And two young cows would investigate the possibility of starting a small petting zoo.

Over the roar of cheers and applause, Deirdre shouted, "But wait, there's more." The animals turned back to her expectantly. "Bull and I decided to modify the rules slightly and name a fourth winner." Finding Stella in the audience, she said to her, "We're intrigued enough with your off-the-cuff idea that we'd like you to come up with a plan for an alpaca yarn business."

"Yes!" Stella high-hoofed the cow standing next to her. This was the kind of challenge she loved! She planned to e-mail Alejandro as soon as she could to share the good news.

Chapter 7

THERE WAS JUST no doubt about it, Deirdre thought. All four business plans on her desk had potential, but Stella's plan for a luxury yarn business was the strongest by far. Deirdre particularly liked that Stella's plan required the smallest investment. The farm had limited resources; only the luxury wool business could be launched from savings. Deirdre hoped luxury wool would be a relatively quick win and that the profits from it might be sufficient to fund entry into one of the other proposed new businesses.

"We'll go with Stella's idea," Deirdre stated. Bull sat across from her on the other side of Marcus's . . . on the other side of *her* desk. Bull had been unusually quiet these past weeks. Was he still brooding that he wasn't running the farm?

"Well, it certainly is an *intriguing* idea," Bull hedged. "But is Stella thinking more with her head . . . or her heart?"

Deirdre ignored the comment. "We'll make the

announcement and celebrate this week and then get moving right away."

Bull's eyes bulged. "Deirdre, slow down. What do you . . . *we* know about alpaca? Who here even heard of an alpaca before this? This plan Stella's concocted *appears* solid, but there are all kinds of risks."

"Yes, Bull, there are risks. It's a new business," said Deirdre.

"This is not the time for something like this." Bull was almost shouting. "You know we're getting squeezed in our core business. That's where we need to keep our focus."

"Bull, we can't win by doing the same thing we always have. We'll just keep getting squeezed."

"We don't know how to do anything else, Deirdre."

"We'll learn."

Bull grimaced. "Well, let's at least consider what could go wrong."

The conversation was making Deirdre nervous. On one hand, she felt it was essential to keep Bull on the farm. On the other, if he was going to do nothing but get in the way. . . .

Deirdre was determined to stay calm. "Stella did that quite well in her plan. And besides, Bull, you're missing the point. Doing *nothing* is the riskiest choice we could make."

Bull stared at the wall above Deirdre's head. She could tell he was trying not to snort. "This could mean the end of the farm," he said. He stomped out, shaking his head.

🐎 🐎 🐎

Deirdre planned the big celebration for Friday night. The contest had been farmtastic, she reassured herself. They had done it. They had found the Big Idea. And she was committed to her course of action.

On Friday afternoon, Deirdre told Stella the good news.

"It just goes to show," Stella beamed, "you never know where your next Big Idea is going to come from."

As Deirdre had hoped, it was a boisterous celebration. There were games, dancing, and a tremendous feast, all under a full moon. Even the losing finalists offered Stella their hearty congratulations.

Stella enjoyed the attention. Deirdre admired how she infused the party with her high energy. She'd brought Peruvian music and pictures to get everyone excited about the arrival of the new and exotic animals. She even led the little animals in two games: sheep, sheep, alpaca, and pin the neck on the alpaca.

After the party, Deirdre made her rounds to check the gates. She trotted along, deep in thought. Luxury wool was a brilliant idea, she felt sure of it. But then, with an arresting thought, Deirdre abruptly stopped her trot. She realized she hadn't given a moment's consideration to what exactly she would do in the morning. It was suddenly very clear to her that **in any great innovation story, the *idea* is only the *beginning*.**

Chapter 8

THE FOLLOWING MORNING, Deirdre set off to find Bull. She wanted to talk with him about what steps they should take next. When she finally spotted him in a far corner of the farm's property, she couldn't believe her eyes. Bull was talking to McGillicuddy, who was perched atop his gigantic tractor. The two appeared to be having a friendly conversation. But what about?

Deirdre returned to her office before Bull could see her. Later, she looked for him again. This time, he was in the barn, puzzling over a tiny dent in a milking machine.

"I've been thinking about *who* should run the new luxury wool business," she said, having decided not to confront Bull about his chat with McGillicuddy.

"Not Stella, I hope," Bull quickly retorted. "She's barely out of school."

"No. I agree with you, Stella's not ready. Actually, I was thinking about Rex."

"No way!" Steam puffed from Bull's nose. "Rex is too important helping with bovine ops. Rex—and Rambo and Rob—all need to stay in their current positions."

"Okay," Deirdre conceded, realizing Bull was right. "So we need somebody not too indispensable to our current operations but nonetheless ready for a real leadership challenge."

As soon as she said this, Deirdre had an idea.

"How about Mav?" she asked.

"Maverick?" Bull tapped his hoof, a habit when he was thinking. "That stallion's a little too sure of himself," Bull mused aloud. "He doesn't have all that much respect for tradition. And, for that matter, he doesn't have all that much experience."

Deirdre waited. Bull was making some good points.

"But all things considered, Mav's probably the best choice," he concluded.

An hour later, the young stallion was standing in Deirdre's office.

"I want you to head up the new luxury wool business," she told him.

What? Mav's jaw dropped. *Run my own business?* It was a very attractive offer. He could call his own shots! And if he succeeded, he could probably skip a promotion or two. In fact, he'd be in the perfect position to suc-

ceed Deirdre. Maybe he'd even be the youngest leader in the farm's history! On the other hand, what did he know about alpaca, other than the fact they were exotic animals—sort of like a camel, sort of like a sheep, really long necks, really fine wool. *Right.* Was he crazy to even consider it?

"Sounds interesting, Deirdre," he said finally, "but also risky. What do you figure the odds of success are?"

"I'm more worried about our odds of survival if we do nothing," Deirdre replied.

"Understood," said Mav. "Let me ask a different question. Given that we are going into uncertain terrain here, Deirdre, how are you going to evaluate me on this project?"

"There are uncertainties to be sure, Mav. If I thought it was an easy project, I wouldn't have called on you. I understand that there are risks."

Mav looked into Deirdre's eyes. He wondered what she would really think if the luxury wool business failed. Then he wondered what she would think of him if he said no.

A few days later, having had time to mull it over, Mav's ambition defeated his anxieties. "I'll take the job!" he told Deirdre.

Deirdre was pleased. "You'll report to Rambo, since luxury wool is most closely tied to ovine ops."

"Fine." Mav had no problem with Rambo.

"You'll need to build your own team," Deirdre continued, "and since the farm doesn't have anyone else available for full-time work right now, you'll have to persuade a few others to pitch in." Deirdre figured that since there hadn't been any shortage of volunteers for the Big

Idea Hunt, Mav shouldn't have any trouble finding animals willing to help.

After the stallion left, Deirdre created a new org chart that formalized Mav's position and tacked it to her bulletin board. The chart looked good, except for one giant invisible question mark: Bull had yet to formally accept her offer to be the farm's chief operating officer.

Just thinking about it made Deirdre nervous.

At the next farm-wide meeting, Deirdre announced Mav's promotion. Mav told the gathered animals he'd be

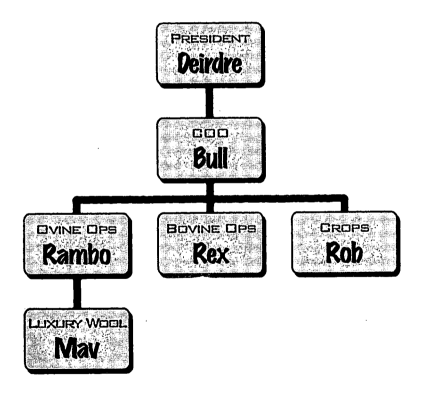

talking to some of them soon about getting involved. Most of the audience seemed excited about the prospect.

Then it was Bull's turn to give his routine update about operations.

"Friends, it's important to understand that our fundamental situation has not changed. The luxury wool business is promising," he stated. "It *might* help us in the *future*. But we can't lose our discipline in managing the *present*. The farm's ongoing cost-cutting initiatives remain critical. In short, the latest numbers show that *we must continue to work harder.*"

The animals looked disheartened. Bull snorted and bounced back and forth on his front hooves. Usually he could charge up the animals, but not today. For weeks, they had been focused on new ideas, innovation, and the future. Now, Bull's speech presented a hard reality. For most in the audience, the future was no different. *Must work harder.*

The next morning, Deirdre found the Count waiting in her office, impatiently tapping a pencil on his beak.

"Deirdre, I just saw the receipt from our corn sales. It's *much* lower than I expected. Did you lock in a price a few months ago as we always do?"

Deirdre had forgotten. She was supposed to have done it around the time of her father's death. This was an untimely error—and a serious one. She thought of the luxury wool start-up. Stella's plan estimated the new business would consume only one-third of the farm's savings before it reached profitability. But that was *before* Deirdre's blunder took a bite out of savings. What if luxury wool's costs were bigger than anticipated? What if it took longer than expected to break even?

The day went from bad to worse. After lunch, McGillicuddy came to see Deirdre in her office. She offered him a seat, trying to hide her anxiety.

"I want to buy the farm, and I'm willing to pay a fair price," said the farmer. He pulled an envelope out of the front pocket of his overalls and put it on Deirdre's desk.

Deirdre looked him squarely in the eye. "The farm is not for sale."

"You'll change your mind," McGillicuddy said. He stood up and left.

Deirdre stared at the envelope sitting on her desk, right next to the dismal corn revenue figures. She was tempted to throw it away, but her curiosity got the better of her. She tore it open.

McGillicuddy surprised her. He really was offering a fair price.

Chapter 9

A FEW WEEKS LATER, Mav sat down with a matronly ewe who served as the farm's purchasing manager. Mav needed her approval before he could sign a contract with the Peruvian alpaca recruiter who had agreed to transport as many alpaca as Mav wanted to hire. It hadn't been easy to find such a recruiter, but now Mav was almost home free.

The purchasing manager, however, had questions. Many questions. She narrowed her eyes at the alpaca photo that Mav had brought with him. "Are these animals well fed?" she demanded. "Are they disease free? How much do you really know about Peru?"

"I'm learning quickly," said Mav. "Give me some credit. I don't even speak Peruvian."

"Spanish."

"Right."

"Is this recruiter certified?" she asked.

"Certified by whom?" Mav replied.

"Mav, did you ask for references? Are you getting the

best possible price? How do you *know* you are getting the best price?"

"Is this really so complicated?" asked Mav.

"Do you have any idea how bad I would look if anything went wrong here? We have standards!" said the manager. "And for good reasons!"

"You know how important this venture is!" Mav retorted. "The future of the farm is at stake! We need to move *quickly*."

"Come back when you have answers," the ewe scolded. "Good day, Mr. Maverick!"

Next, Mav walked into an office with the letters AR on the door—animal resources. The director invited him to sit down. She had raised fourteen foals in her lifetime, so little surprised her . . . until now.

"I'm shocked, just shocked with these alpaca salary requirements," she said. "All they do is grow wool!"

"*Luxury* wool!" Mav corrected. "And alpaca salaries were itemized in the business plan!"

"Nobody asked me to review the plan."

Mav looked agitated, but the director continued. "How do you think the sheep will feel when they find out the alpaca are being paid nearly twice their salaries?"

"They won't find out," Mav argued.

"Mav, please. If there's one thing I've learned over my years in AR, it's that everyone knows how much everyone else is getting paid."

Later that day, Mav met with the Count, who had actually summoned him to his office. The Count wanted to discuss Mav's proposal for a new website.

"We've built websites before," said the Count, "but

they have *never* cost this much. These expenses were not in the plan."

"We didn't anticipate the added cost of producing a *first-rate* graphic design. We're in a luxury business. We have to *look* the part."

"Mav, I cannot approve this. I have an operating margin to hit this quarter. If I'm off by so much as one-tenth of 1 percent, Bull will be furious!"

Mav's last scheduled appointment was with Maisie, who had promised him mock-ups for a luxury wool brochure. Because Maisie was the only fashion-conscious

animal on the farm, and because she loved reading glamour magazines, it seemed only natural that she should help with marketing.

"So, let's see what you've got," said Mav.

Maisie fiddled with the flower in her summer bonnet. "Mav, you *know* I'd like nothing better than to draw *bee-ewe-tee-full* sketches for your brochure," she said. "But we're all under incredible pressure. I've had *zero* free time. And Bull has been a bear!"

The meeting with Maisie left Mav feeling dejected. Everywhere he'd gone, he'd run into obstacles. For the first time in his life, he experienced a real fear of failure. Reluctantly, he sought out Rambo to ask for help.

Rambo listened as Mav explained what kind of day he'd had.

"I'll see what I can do," Rambo said. He still wasn't convinced luxury wool was the future of the farm, but he had promised Deirdre he would support Mav.

Two weeks later, both Mav and Rambo sat down with Deirdre for a routine progress report. Both were nervous. The simple truth was they had no progress to report.

Deirdre, who rarely showed her temper, stood so forcefully that her chair swiveled twice behind her. "Why aren't the animals pitching in?" she demanded. "Didn't I make it clear that this new business is important? Didn't I make it clear that the future of the farm depends on it?"

Mav left the room feeling chastised, a feeling he couldn't stand. Somehow, someway, he was going to move the luxury wool business forward . . . even if it meant breaking some rules!

Back in his office, Mav called the Peruvian recruiter

and made arrangements to hire a dozen working alpaca. He thought he was in the clear, but the recruiter sent a fax to confirm the order, and Bull just happened to be standing right next to the fax machine. Seconds later, Mav was staring eyeball-to-eyeball at a very angry Bull.

Later that evening, Mav was still stinging from Bull's tongue-lashing. For his part, Bull was steaming at Mav's audacity. Just how far would this stallion go in the name of luxury wool? How much would get destroyed in the process? And would Deirdre be cheering him on the whole way?

Bull made a decision. He picked up the phone and dialed McGillicuddy.

Part 2

Chapter 10

EIRDRE SPENT THE morning talking with as many animals as she could about luxury wool. Everyone reaffirmed its importance to the farm. So, why weren't they doing anything to support Mav?

Deirdre asked question after question, pressuring the animals until she got to the truth. Eventually, she understood what the animals couldn't quite articulate. Yes, they all understood that luxury wool was important. *But the core business was more important.*

And why wouldn't it be? The animals were evaluated, paid, and promoted based on how well they performed in *today's* business, not some future hypothetical possibility. And they all were well aware that if they let up on their workload or divided their attentions even briefly, the farm's financials would deteriorate even further. Bull reminded them of it every day!

It was clear now to Deirdre that the animals weren't lazy or resistant to change. They were *good animals* doing *good work.* They were doing everything they could to keep the farm's business as healthy as possible. And that important realization clarified Deirdre's understanding of the challenge she faced. Somehow, she had to both build a new business and sustain excellence in the existing one . . . *simultaneously.*

Deirdre had never put much stock in business books. She was more a believer in the school of hard knocks than the musings of the ivory tower. This challenge, however, was completely new to her. She went online and ordered several books to be shipped overnight.

Much of what she read over the next several days seemed like common sense dressed up with fancy, coined terms. Many of the books focused on techniques for finding just the right idea—she had a great idea—or on the need to classify various innovation initiatives—she had just one that she needed to move forward *right now*. But in the books that did apply to her situation, all the authors seemed to emphasize one particular point: Deirdre needed to create a *dedicated team* for the new business and she needed to act as Mav's "sponsor."

Deirdre liked the logic of this advice. Mav had run into conflict everywhere he went for help. Ultimately, the conflict was between Bull and Mav—the present versus the future. Mav was capable, to be sure, but he had nothing close to Bull's influence with the animals. It was hardly a fair fight!

Deirdre realized that **expecting one leader to "just go make it happen" was a woefully inadequate approach to moving an innovative idea forward.**

The next week, Deirdre called Rambo and Mav into her office. "Mav, from now on you'll report directly to me, not Rambo" she said. Mav nodded.

"Any problem with this, Rambo?" Deirdre held her breath. You just never knew how a ram might react.

"Are you kidding me? I'm more than happy focusing just on ovine ops." Rambo was thrilled to drop the burden of a project that only seemed to bring him headaches.

"Mav," Deirdre said, turning her attention back to the stallion, "I've decided you need a dedicated team to move things forward."

"Great!" Mav was enthusiastic. More resources were exactly what he thought he needed.

"Figure out who you need," Deirdre said, "and I'll make the arrangements."

Within a day, Mav reported back to her. "I want Maisie to head up marketing," he said. "She may seem flighty at times, but she's got a passion for luxury and high fashion and, well, years of experience wearing fine wool."

"Go on," Deirdre said.

"I want my brother Matt for sales."

"But he's even younger than you."

"Matt has an amazing gift for persuasion," Mav explained. "I can't tell you how many times when we were colts that he convinced me to help him with his math homework, and then I ended up doing it for him!"

"All right," Deirdre conceded. "Who else?"

"I want Max over in ovine ops to manage manufacturing. He's down in the yarn production shop every chance he gets. He knows and loves machines."

Deirdre saw the logic of this last choice, though she knew it wouldn't sit well with Rambo—or with Bull.

Sure enough, when Deirdre told Bull about Mav's team, he went bull-istic. "Deirdre, you can't do this! How can you strip me of three of my most important workers?"

Deirdre managed to convince Bull that he could do without Maisie. She was incredibly productive but just one in a herd. Matt and Max were another story. Despite Deirdre's best efforts to convince Bull that he could quickly train replacements, she couldn't mollify him. Once again, he stormed out of her office.

Deirdre looked at the painting of her father on the wall. Having Marcus watch over her shoulder while she worked offered some modicum of reassurance. Despite Bull's angry protests as well as the risks, she still believed she was making the right move for the farm, so long as this luxury wool venture proved a relatively quick success.

Chapter 11

"DO YOU HAVE a second?" Bull had already entered Deirdre's office. "It's really important."

Deirdre sighed at the unexpected visit. "Of course, Bull." Her stomach knotted. She thought again of the bull's all-too-friendly chat with McGillicuddy. If Bull was resigning, should she try to convince him to stay or just let him go? Did she really have any control over the matter anyway?

"I said no," Bull announced.

"You said no?" Deirdre's heart beat faster.

"I said no to the other offers. Three farms offered me great jobs. McGillicuddy wanted to make me the number two manager on his farm, a much bigger responsibility than what I have here at Windsor. But I said no."

"You said no?" Deirdre realized she was repeating herself.

"Windsor is my home—and my family. And you need me, Deirdre. I'm saying yes to *you*. Yes, I'll be your chief operating officer."

"Huh?"

Bull smiled. He enjoyed seeing the mare at a rare loss for words.

"I want the farm to succeed, Deirdre," Bull continued, "and I believe the best way to help the farm is by continuing to work harder. I'm committed to the only principles I've ever known: *Faster. Stronger. More efficient.*" He looked Deirdre directly in the eye. "I'll be honest, Deirdre. I don't feel any better about luxury wool. But, truthfully, I haven't been able to come up with a good answer to your argument that doing nothing is the biggest risk of all."

"I see," said Deirdre. She was surprised by the admission.

"So I'm staying."

Deirdre felt an enormous sense of relief. Despite her disagreements with Bull, he was a critical asset to the farm—and a good friend. She came from behind her desk and tried to give him a hug.

"Deirdre, never hug a bull."

"Right," she said.

When Deirdre called the farm-wide meeting to order a half hour after she'd met with Bull, she felt lighter than she had for a long time. The feeling didn't last very long.

Addressing the crowd, she stressed the importance of giving Windsor's luxury wool business sufficient freedom and space to grow. "All of us are going to have to be more flexible," she said. "Luxury wool is a different kind of business for Windsor. We're going to have to change the way we work. I'm going to be more involved, making sure we're making the right choices.

"Mav will be reporting directly to me," she continued. Several animals tittered at this news. "And Maisie,

Matt, and Max are going to be working on luxury wool full-time." More rumbles sounded through the audience and not, Deirdre suspected, because it was almost lunchtime.

Deirdre unveiled the revised organizational chart.

"Deirdre, these are tough times," one of the sheep piped up. "We're all working overtime just to keep the farm profitable. Now you're taking three good workers from us. That will increase the pressure!"

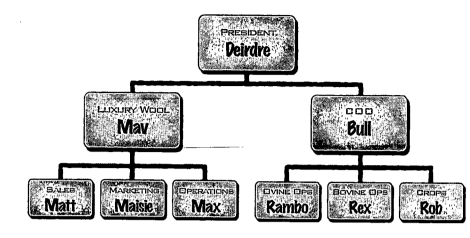

"Losing three good workers is hard," Deirdre acknowledged. "But we'll make some new hires and early promotions. There is no avoiding the fact that as a company, *we have to find a way to do two very different things at the same time.* We have to sustain excellence in the existing business *and* build a new and uncertain one. Bull will be talking with many of you about how to minimize the disruption."

After the meeting, Deirdre overheard three ewes gossiping around the water trough. "Well, it certainly seems to me that Deirdre is playing favorites," said one. "Why is Mav—and Mav alone—allowed to handpick a team, damn the consequences?"

"Marcus must be rolling over in his grave," said another. "He was always scrupulously egalitarian."

"I wonder what that charismatic stallion did to get so close to Deirdre?" whispered the third. "Maybe some naughty nuzzling late at night?"

Deirdre sighed and trotted off in the opposite direction. She knew that even the best animals sometimes succumbed to gossip and petty jealousies, especially during times of stress.

Deirdre had other concerns. Life on Windsor Farm was about to get even more interesting. Mav had informed her that the first dozen alpaca would arrive the very next week.

Chapter 12

DEIRDRE CALLED STELLA into her office. She knew the young ewe had been disappointed about not being involved in the luxury wool business. After all, it had been her idea. But Deirdre had other plans for her protégé. To provide exposure to all of the farm's operations, Deirdre had created a special rotation program for Stella—six months in each of the three major divisions, starting with crops. But now, things needed to be adjusted.

"I'm going to move you from crops to ovine operations, effective immediately," Deirdre said. "Your foremost responsibility will be to support Rambo."

"Whatever I can do to help." Stella loved getting special attention from Deirdre.

"The alpaca are about to arrive at Windsor Farm," Deirdre continued. "You're comfortable with them. I want you to help the other sheep feel comfortable, too."

"No problem." Stella was happy to be given such an important job. The only downside was that the assignment would make her think even more about Alejandro. Maintaining a long-distance relationship was proving harder than she had imagined.

The very next day, she and Mav, with Matt's help, persuaded all the animals to gather for a welcoming celebration. On the morning of the herd's arrival, Stella sported the scarf Alejandro had given her as a present. She hung a huge sign that said, WELCOME ALPACA. She set out the special cake she had baked (and Maisie had insisted on decorating). She double-checked to make sure everything was in order with the hay buffet. The other farm animals mingled around the building in anticipation.

Finally, a long truck pulled up by the barn. The driver opened the doors and, tentatively, the alpaca walked down the ramp. They looked exhausted and wary.

"Welcome!" Stella called out.

Some of the Windsor animals cheered. Others looked apprehensive.

Stella walked up to a fawn-colored alpaca and shook her hoof. "I'm Stella. Nice to meet you."

She motioned for one of the more outgoing sheep to follow suit. The ram approached a gray alpaca and looked up—*way up*. The alpaca extended his head forward and downward as best he could. *"Hola,"* he said.

The sheep jumped back, clearly intimidated, and ran toward the pasture. The other sheep, being sheep, followed.

Stella knew what everyone was thinking:. Were these strange creatures really the future of the farm?

Meanwhile, Mav's internal tensions were running

silo-high. Ever since Deirdre had announced the organizational changes, the animals had been giving him a hard time. "Oh, reporting straight to Deirdre now. Isn't *that* special!" Rex had ribbed. And when Mav had tried to secure some good grazing land for the new arrivals, Rambo had sharply nixed the idea. He wouldn't allow the alpaca to graze alongside the sheep. Because of the grief Mav had been getting from the other animals about "special treatment," he decided not to push it or ask Deirdre to intervene.

After lunch, Mav asked the alpaca to follow him.

One of the alpaca noticed they were following a path marked by a sign: THE BACK FORTY. He pointed out the sign to a friend walking alongside him. "What do you think it means?" he asked. The friend shrugged.

A few days after the alpaca arrived, Mav and Max decided to shear one of the herd ahead of schedule. They wanted to test how well the farm's yarn-making machinery worked with alpaca wool. The pair visited Rambo to schedule the test.

"You expect to use my yarn-making equipment?" Rambo's tone had an edge. "I thought you were running your own show, Mav, especially now that you have your own team and report directly to Deirdre."

"Rambo, don't tell me you expect the farm to buy more equipment," Mav countered. "That's an expensive investment we can't afford right now. Plus, it would take me forever to put together a new shop from scratch!"

"I can't afford any interruptions," Rambo insisted, "especially with sheep-shearing season right around the corner! Why don't you just lease some equipment?"

Mav wanted to knock the ram's block off, but he had learned a thing or two from his brother about persuasive sales tactics. "Rambo, buddy, c'mon. You run one of the best yarn-making operations in the region. You know it would be a lot more efficient for us to combine efforts."

Rambo was unmoved. As he enumerated his objections, Stella walked in and interrupted, clearly upset.

"I'm worried about the alpaca," she said. "Some of them are losing weight and many of them seem depressed. They may be accustomed to rocky terrain, but The Back Forty just doesn't have enough food for them. And they need more space to roam. In my opinion, they're totally stressed out."

"Aren't we all," Mav muttered. "Aren't we all!" He knew the time had come to get Deirdre more involved.

That night, Deirdre was working late, long after she had put Russell and Thomas to bed. Earlier, she had listened to Mav and Rambo repeat their arguments about sharing—or not sharing—the grazing land and yarn-making machinery. Stella, who often burned the midnight oil herself, happened to walk past Deirdre's open door.

"Have a minute?" Deirdre called out to her. "I'd like your opinion."

Stella smiled. The *leader of the farm* was asking *her* for input.

"Mav says you told him that the alpaca aren't doing well in The Back Forty. What do you think we should do?"

Stella didn't hesitate. "Has anyone considered the obvious? Have the sheep and alpaca share *both* the sheep's existing land *and* The Back Forty."

"Sheep and alpaca, living together?" Deirdre asked. As soon as she had uttered the question, she couldn't help but laugh. Stella obviously thought it could work.

"I'm *positive* it can work," Stella assured Deirdre.

Later, as Deirdre performed her nightly gate check, she reflected on her decision to create a dedicated team for luxury wool. She had thought that once the team was in place, the business would naturally accelerate. Instead, there were *new* disagreements.

Mav had run into conflicts when he did something imminently sensible: he had tried to make the best use of the farm's existing assets, like its grazing land and yarn-making equipment. Deirdre realized that Mav's dedicated team couldn't succeed as an *independent* team. Mav needed help. The team running the core business had to be involved.

The next day, Deirdre created a new organizational chart. She went over the changes face-to-face with Bull, Rambo, Mav, and Max to be extra certain they all were on the same page. Mav's sales and marketing teams would still operate independently, but from this point forward, all sheep care, alpaca care, and yarn production would be managed as a joint operation.

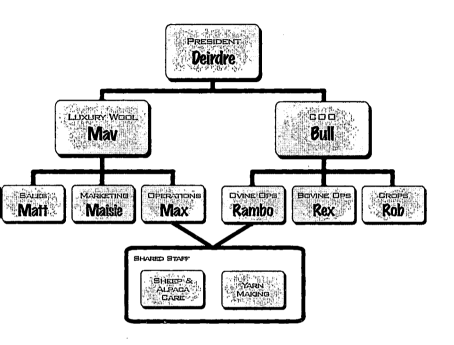

87

Will the sheep save the farm?

Will the alpaca save the farm?

Chapter 13

RAMBO GRUMBLED TO himself the entire walk to The Back Forty. What a pain, he thought, pulling open the gates that divided the sheep pasture from the alpaca's rocky grazing land. Whoever heard of sheep and alpaca living together?! This could only mean trouble.

But neither group budged an acre, or even an inch. The sheep, nervous about the alpaca, stayed in the sheep pasture. The alpaca, nervous about the sheep, stayed in The Back Forty.

"Those alpaca spit all the time," the sheep whispered among themselves. It was true. It was the one camelid habit Stella had struggled to accept while she was in Peru.

"Those sheep poop everywhere," the alpaca complained to each other. "At least we do our business all in one place."

Seeing the separate herds, Stella knew she had her work cut out for her. Later, as she sat in her cubicle, pondering how to bring the two groups together, her mind drifted to Alejandro.

89

"*Stellalalala!*" It was Maisie, twirling about to show off a bee-ewe-tee-full new dress. But her friend's mind was somewhere else. "Stella! What are you daydreaming about?"

"Alejandro," Stella sighed. "I was thinking about how easily we bonded."

"Really? Do tell," Maisie said.

"Alejandro hates cold nights after getting sheared— just like I do," Stella explained. "And he gets bored eating grass all of the time—just like I do. And he likes to be around others. Just like I do."

"Oh, how romantic," Maisie cooed.

And that's when it hit Stella. She needed to show the sheep and alpaca how much they had in common. She just knew they could get along fine if they simply understood one another.

So Stella met with the sheep and explained to them that the alpaca were gentle creatures, and though they preferred to be among their own kind, once you got to know them they were really quite wonderful. Then she met with the alpaca, telling them the sheep were mellow, easy to get along with, and that they tended to move around in droves. She spent hours making introductions between the two groups.

Pretty soon, the animals warmed to one another—so much so that they exchanged some good-natured ribbing.

"How's the weather down there," the alpaca teased the sheep.

"We may not have long necks," the sheep retorted, "but we produce *two* products for the farm: wool *and* milk. You alpaca are just one-trick . . . camelids."

Rambo had to admit, things were working out. Combining care of sheep and alpaca proved much easier than he had expected. Adding a dozen alpaca really was no different from adding a dozen sheep. "I'm pleasantly surprised," Rambo made a point to tell Mav.

"I told you, buddy." The stallion grinned, greatly relieved. Maybe, he thought, the tension between the two of them was over.

It wasn't. In fact, their relationship soon became quite a bit more tangled.

A few days later, Rambo walked into his yarn-making facility, expecting to see the usual order and efficiency. Instead, he nearly tore out his horns. The place was a disaster. Piles of snarled yarn cluttered the shop floor. Machines were jammed. His manufacturing team looked frantic.

"What's going on here?" he demanded.

"It's this darn alpaca wool," the foresheep snapped. "We're not equipped to handle this type of fiber and all these varieties."

"What are you talking about? What varieties?" Rambo asked.

The foresheep wiped some sweat from his brow. "Alpaca fibers differ depending on the animal's lineage and depending on what part of the animal the fiber comes from. Plus, you have to keep each grade and weight of wool completely separate because, apparently, they command really different prices."

Rambo groaned.

"Plus," the foresheep continued, "the most expensive grades of alpaca fiber are unbelievably delicate to process. The yarn easily splits or frays if it's not handled

just so. That means a lighter touch on the machinery. Which means we constantly have to reset the machines or do some steps manually. Should I go on?"

"I've heard enough," Rambo replied, and he shut down production for the day.

Stella witnessed the entire debacle in the yarn-making facility. With production at a halt, she contacted Alejandro. *Help!* she texted him. *Do you know any experts in making alpaca yarn?*

Five minutes later, she got a reply. *I'll set up a call with my uncle. He's been in textiles all his life.*

After the call, Stella understood the problem.

Rambo's operation was geared toward turning bulk commodity sheep wool into yarn in the most efficient way possible. The team included specialists that handled each step in the process—separating, skirting, washing, teasing, carding, roving, spinning, winding, finishing, and shipping.

But in Peru, textile producers specialized not by *step in the process,* but by *product.* Alejandro's uncle, for example, had specialists for different grades and weights—for basic, everyday alpaca wool; sort-of-luxurious alpaca wool; finest-in-the-world alpaca wool; and so forth. Each specialist carried batches of wool through the entire process.

Stella immediately recognized the implications. There was no way to organize Rambo's team in two different ways at the same time. Even a small step in that direction would be extremely disruptive to existing operations.

Stella hurried to tell Rambo and Mav what she had learned. She found the two of them in a heated discussion. "There's just no way we'll ever succeed in combining yarn-making operations," Rambo was shouting. "It's too much trouble!"

"We've been over this! We can't afford a separate shop!" Mav was frustrated. Why was combining yarn making so much harder than combining animal care?

Stella attempted to defuse the situation by explaining what she had learned. Mav, though tightly wound at the moment, seemed to understand. He later agreed that a dedicated production facility, while expensive, really was a necessity.

Soon, Mav made the proposal to Deirdre, who listened carefully and asked several questions. She saw there was just no getting around the necessity of **assigning activities that were beyond the narrow, specialized capabilities of her existing organization to the dedicated team.** The thought of these additional expenditures worried her deeply, but there was no choice. She approved Mav's request for a separate manufacturing facility.

That night, as the colts watched their favorite reality show, *So You Think You Can Prance,* Deirdre updated the org chart once again.

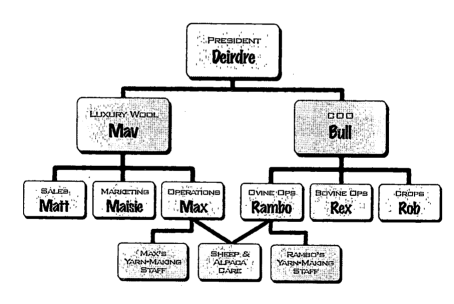

Chapter 14

SEVERAL WEEKS AFTER Deirdre approved the new manu-facturing facility, she arrived at her office to find the Count pacing in front of her door. Deirdre invited him in, but he refused to sit down. This day, no fewer than five pencils were stashed beneath his wing.

"We need to talk about the farm's cash flow and sav-ings balance," he gobbled. "As best I can tell, we still have sufficient runway to get this luxury wool business off the ground—but just barely."

"I know," Deirdre said. "I'm working on it."

Deirdre felt she needed a backup plan, something to help the farm get by if the luxury wool business failed. After the turkey trotted off, Deirdre picked up the phone. It was time to set up more appointments with bankers and investors. It wasn't going to be easy to persuade any of them to take a risk on Windsor Farm, but she had to try.

Meanwhile, Mav, Matt, and Maisie were just arriving at a meeting of their own, this one with a human named Lucinda, their first prospective customer. Max had the new yarn-making operations up and running, so Mav had turned his attention to sales and marketing.

"May I take your coats?" Lucinda asked as the trio entered the woman's elegantly appointed office.

"Isn't mine gorgeous?" Maisie gushed, almost knocking over an expensive-looking vase when she twirled to show off her alpaca wrap. Despite the warm weather, Maisie had insisted that she, Mav, and Matt all wear clothing made from Windsor's alpaca wool.

"So, I understand you'll be able to offer new luxury wool soon?" Lucinda got right down to business.

Maisie hurriedly slid the glossy sales brochure she had created across the desktop. The brochure featured her own ideas for luxury alpaca wool creations—coats, pants, sweaters, and hats, most of the items sporting fancy flourishes. "Imagine your customers wearing fashions like these!" she said.

Both Mav and Matt had agreed that Maisie's brochure would make a great first impression, as would actual samples of their quality product.

Lucinda glanced at the brochure, then turned to Mav. "Tell me about your yarn-making operation."

Before Mav could respond, Maisie jumped in, unable to contain her enthusiasm. "This is the softest wool you've ever put your hands on. Feel it!" She yanked Matt's scarf off his neck and handed it to Lucinda. "Imagine how good you would look in this!" Maisie pointed to a design in the brochure of a shawl with a floral flourish.

Lucinda pointedly ignored Maisie. "Tell me about your yarn-making operation," she said to Mav.

"Currently, we are producing three different grades of alpaca yarn," Mav replied.

"Can you dye the yarn any color?" Lucinda demanded. "Can you handle custom orders? . . . What's the largest volume you can ship at one time? . . . How quickly can you ship? . . ."

Mav felt he answered everything satisfactorily.

After the meeting, Lucinda asked to speak with him privately. "I like Maisie. She's charming," she said, although her tone conveyed exactly the opposite. "But we have our own fashion designers here. And they are really good."

As Matt drove the group back to the farm and Maisie sketched in her fashion notebook, Mav took another look at Maisie's glossy brochure. This time, he tried to see it through the customer's eyes. His customers were manufacturers, not fashion-conscious consumers. Mav considered the possibility that Maisie's years spent reading fashion magazines and wearing wool hats didn't provide the kind of experience he needed. He decided to ask Stella to help him do some research.

The two worked late that night. Mav brewed another pot of strong alfalfa tea as he and Stella pored over articles in the Peruvian textile industry trade press. Mav was grateful that Stella had learned quite a bit of Spanish while traveling.

"Mav, look at this!" Stella translated the headline "Luxury Wool Marketer of the Year." The article included a picture of the award winner, Andrea, a mature, elegantly dressed alpaca with a rather haughty expression. Mav and Stella agreed they should call her for advice. When they did the next day, the conversation took a most unexpected turn.

After the call, Mav hurried to find Deirdre to share his and Stella's idea.

"You want to do what?" Deirdre asked, dumbfounded.

"We want to bring a Peruvian alpaca into the management team," Mav repeated. He told her how Lucinda had reacted to Maisie and how he had concluded that Maisie was in over her head. And now, by sheer good luck and timing, Peru's Luxury Wool Marketer of the Year was interested in coming to work at Windsor!

"She wants to live abroad," Mav explained.

"I just don't know," said Deirdre. "It's one thing to have working alpaca on the farm. But to add one to the management team? It seems like a big step away from the ideal of a family business."

"There isn't anyone else on the farm who could do better," Mav insisted.

Later that night, Deirdre was tucking in Thomas for the night when the colt asked if he could go to architecture camp that summer. "What about bug camp?" she asked. Only a short while ago, her younger son thought it would be cool to be an entomologist. "We'll talk about it in the morning," she promised.

Deirdre set off to check the gates, using the time as usual for reflection. She thought about her boys. Thomas was so different from his older brother, Russell. Russell had known forever that he wanted to work on the farm, just like his mom and grandpa. Maybe that was why Deirdre felt completely in her comfort zone as she prepared Russell for adulthood. She knew so much about what he needed to do and learn. Parenting Thomas, however, was different. She couldn't be nearly so directive. All she could do was try to be sure that he had good experiences and was surrounded by good role models.

And then Deirdre thought, What if raising a luxury wool business was much like raising Thomas? It made some sense. Whatever the script was for building the new business, it wasn't in Windsor's history. It couldn't be ferreted out from Deirdre's direct experience. Luxury wool was entirely different.

The reality, she saw, was that **building a dedicated team is much like building a new and different company from the ground up.** She did not know exactly how the dedicated team should operate. She couldn't direct every detail and neither could Mav. She could only try to get the right individuals involved and create the right conditions for success. And that meant, for starters, that she needed to hire the best candidates she could find, not just settle for whomever was available on Windsor Farm.

🐎 🐎 🐎

It took Andrea ten days to relocate to Windsor Farm, which was exactly the same amount of time Maisie spent crying over the news that she'd been replaced as the team's luxury wool marketer. Deirdre and Mav had sat down with her on the front steps of the farmhouse to break the news.

"You'll always be a crucial member of our family," Deirdre had reassured her prize milk producer.

"We'll find ways to keep you involved in luxury wool," Mav added.

Maisie just sobbed even harder, throwing her glossy brochures to the ground.

And Maisie wasn't the only one throwing things. Once Andrea had learned the operation under the tutelage of Mav, Matt, and Max, she started throwing her weight around.

"Max, why are you producing only three different products?" she demanded. "Our customers are going to want lots of gradations—different weights, different degrees of softness, and lots of price points."

Max sighed. How many times did he have to explain things to this alpaca? "Andrea, the fewer products we produce, the more efficient our operation is. You've seen the farm. You've seen how tightly we operate. That's why we're successful. That's why we're still in business."

Andrea sighed. How many times did she have to explain things to this ram? "Max, the cost of the yarn isn't the be-all and end-all. At the luxury end of the market, cost isn't the most important factor—or even the second or third most important. The most important factor is that we deliver what customers want."

Andrea also confronted Matt, showing him a list of hundreds of small apparel makers that focused on high-end woolen clothing. "How many of these folks have you communicated with about the wonders of alpaca?" she asked.

"What's the point?" Matt asked. "Those companies are tiny. If we just get a few of the biggies, we'll be all set."

"That's how it works with *sheep* wool," Andrea said. "You sell direct to a few big customers and a few big distributors. Small shops buy from the distributors. But there are no distributors of alpaca wool. It's too small a market to interest them. We're going to have to go direct to the small designers."

Matt looked at Andrea like she was having a senior moment. "Where do you think I'm going to find time to visit all these small designers?"

"Quite obviously, *Matt*, you'll need to hire a small sales force."

"That's expensive and probably unnecessary!"

"At the luxury end of the market, cost isn't the first consideration—or even the second or third!" Andrea wondered if anyone had been listening to her since she'd arrived. "What's more," she continued, "the small apparel makers make up more than two-thirds of the market."

Having made her point *again*, Andrea dramatically tossed her elegant scarf over her shoulder and strutted away. Despite being an alpaca of good breeding, she felt so frustrated she could spit.

— — — — — — · — — —

Will Andrea save the farm?

Chapter 15

MAV CONSULTED WITH Deirdre about the standoff between Andrea and Matt and Max. What should he do?

After thinking about it for a while, Deirdre concluded that while Andrea wouldn't win any popularity contests on the farm, she *was* an expert marketer of alpaca yarn. Her ideas seemed sound. She conveyed her thoughts to Mav.

Mav told Max and Matt that from then on, Andrea would select target customers and make decisions about the breadth of the product line. Matt and Max nodded but both were uncomfortable. It was never easy to give up control.

🐎 🐎 🐎

Six months later, Windsor Farm was shipping alpaca yarn every day. Orders were growing steadily. To keep up with demand, Mav was hiring more and more alpaca. They now were almost as numerous as sheep.

Deirdre made a point to stop by the community board outside of the alpaca yarn shop every morning to read the customer testimonials Mav posted.

Best sweater I've ever worn!

So soft!

Amazing quality!

World class!

-Mav really seemed to have the new business pointed in the right direction. For the first time in a long while, Deirdre felt she could devote more of her attention elsewhere and let Mav handle the day-to-day operations of luxury wool.

Before long, however, new troubles emerged. The farm was unaccustomed to such rapid growth. Mav and Rambo hadn't adequately planned for the arrival of so many alpaca. The pastures were getting crowded. Mav was pressuring the caretakers to tend to the needs of the alpaca. Rambo was insisting they tend to the needs of the sheep.

Making matters worse, some of the alpaca started acting cocky after Mav posted the reviews, believing too much in their own press. This was especially true of Alvin, a recent arrival who loved to tease the sheep.

"Feel it and weep!" Alvin flaunted his super thick wool. "That is what world-class, top-notch luxury wool feels like, my friend."

Another time, Alvin stood atop a knoll. "Look up here!" he yelled to three sheep below him. "How does it feel to look at the *future of the farm*!" Alvin grinned from ear to ear.

One day, Stella heard a shouting match in the sheep pasture. "Take it back!" one of the sheep bleated, shoving an alpaca.

"What's the matter, *dinosheep*?" the alpaca taunted. "Afraid with all of us superior alpaca around you'll go extinct one day?"

The sheep were peeved. It was one thing when there were just a few alpaca around. It was one thing when the whole ordeal seemed to be nothing more than a quirky little experiment. But now these overbearing alpaca were everywhere. And if there was one thing that infuriated the sheep to no end it was the way the alpaca *always seemed to be looking down on them*!

The tensions only got worse. After one particularly ugly interaction, the sheep herded themselves into an angry mob on one side of the pasture. The alpaca did the same on the other side. Both sides seemed eager for a brawl.

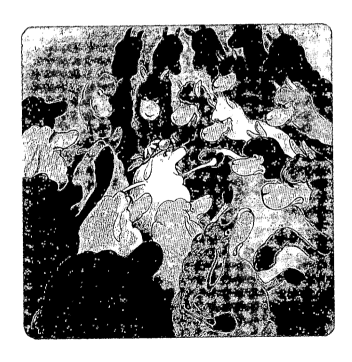

Stella, who had been trying to negotiate a peace agreement, knew she had to act fast. She inserted herself between the factions and started her appeal. Though she was as spirited as ever, she could tell her efforts were falling short. Finally, she resorted to simple bribery.

"Cookies!" she shouted, racing around the pasture. The sheep looked excited but the alpaca seemed confused. *"Galletas! Galletas!"* Stella realized the alpaca did not yet understand the word *cookie*. "Free cookies—galletas—for every animal that grazes peacefully for the rest of the day."

And with that, an all-out war between the alpaca and sheep was averted . . . for the moment.

Later that evening, Stella felt satisfied. She was making a real difference on the farm, and she had managed to defuse a tense situation. But there was a downside to her success. She had to postpone an overdue phone call to Alejandro so she could spend the evening baking cookies.

Not twenty-four hours later, the sheep and alpaca were at it again. Stella's cookies had proven only a temporary fix.

Mav was discouraged. He decided to ask his boss for help. Deirdre asked Rambo and Bull to join Mav and her in her office. Bull noticed Marcus's portrait and felt a sudden stab of sadness. Boy, oh boy, he missed the good old days when life was simpler, and when *faster, stronger, and more efficient* had been enough.

The meeting quickly became tense. "Either the sheep have to go or the alpaca have to go—one or the other," Rambo opened abruptly. "And, Deirdre, you know who has been here longer! You know who your real family is!"

Bull added, "It's true, Deirdre. The alpaca are constant disruptions. We can't have that."

Mav's ears twitched. He couldn't believe what he was hearing. "We all agreed to build this new business. We can't possibly walk away now, just when we're showing real signs of success! There has to be a solution!"

A few days later, Deirdre felt that she'd found just that—a solution. She sought out Rambo in the sheep pasture. He was breaking up yet another scuffle between a sheep and an alpaca. She waited while he wiped spit from his muzzle.

"I spoke with our friend Baxter, the horse that runs Chelsea Farms down the road," Deirdre said. "He's agreed, for a fee, to allow some of our sheep to graze in his pastures."

"But that's going to cost us money!" Rambo argued. "And my bonus is based on my profit margins!"

"I'll adjust your bonus so you're unaffected," Deirdre reassured him.

"The sheep won't like it," Rambo muttered.

"The sheep will understand," Deirdre smiled, "if a talented ram like you explains it clearly." She had learned long ago that it was easy to flatter a ram.

Suddenly, another commotion erupted in the field.

"Shove over, fuzz face."

"Ow!"

"Get your hooves off of me!"

Deirdre saw that an alpaca had a sheep's head pinned to the ground. She galloped over to intervene.

"You will both stop this now!" she commanded, staring down at the alpaca kneeling over the helpless sheep.

The alpaca wasn't accustomed to being looked down upon, nor was he accustomed to attention from the leader of the farm. She seemed *very mad.*

Deirdre climbed atop a bale of hay, a better vantage point from which to address the alpaca and sheep clustered in the field. "For days now," she said, "I've been hearing nothing but unhappiness from these pastures. To some degree, I understand it. We've learned just how different luxury wool is. And yes, you alpaca are rather unique animals. And yes, it's been crowded lately."

Deirdre slowly surveyed the crowd to make sure she had everyone's complete attention.

"But all of you have lost sight of the most important fact. *You are both on the same team.* You both need each other. Alpaca, do you know where the money that we are using to build the luxury wool business is coming from? In great part, it's coming from the sale of sheep's milk and sheep's wool! And perhaps you've forgotten, but you all graze on sheep pasture!"

The alpaca hung their fuzzy heads.

"Sheep, do you recall why we brought the alpaca on the farm in the first place? Because we simply cannot continue to exist as a family farm unless we succeed in building new businesses."

The sheep looked rattled.

"Do you know who visited the farm yesterday?" Deirdre pressed on, raising her pitch. "McGillicuddy! He's putting more pressure on us. He insists if we don't agree to sell Windsor Farm to him now, he'll get it for a song a year or two from now . . . when we are in real trouble. And he might be right."

The sheep now looked terrified. They *definitely* did not want to get bought out by McGillicuddy! That would be very *baaaaad*.

The alpaca also understood the gravity of the situation. Even Alvin, the most self-important alpaca of them all, looked . . . well . . . sheepish.

Deirdre hopped off the hay bale, confident she had made her point. Like it or not, she realized, she could not disengage from the day-to-day concerns of luxury wool. Her role was vital. **Conflicts were inevitable**, she saw. **Nonetheless, nurturing a healthy partnership between the dedicated team and the existing organization was essential.**

Chapter 16

MONDAY MORNING, BRIGHT and early, two office phones rang almost simultaneously. Stella picked hers up on the first ring.

"Alejandro! What a wonderful surprise!" She looked at the framed photo on her desk, smiling at Alejandro's handsome face.

"Stella, I have a proposal to make," he said.

"Proposal?" Her heart raced.

"I want you to come live with me in Peru."

"Oh my!" was all Stella could manage. She wasn't expecting this. Or was she?

"It's just too hard to live without you," Alejandro said.

Stella shared the sentiment, but her emotions were mixed. "What would I *do* in Peru?" she wondered aloud.

"What do you mean?"

"I mean, what would I do all day? Every day? We wouldn't be hiking the Inca Trail, you know."

"You could do whatever you wanted. But, Stella, you

wouldn't even have to work if you didn't want to. I just got promoted. We'd be fine."

Stella promised to think about it.

The other Monday morning phone call was for Deirdre. It was her banker.

"While your new luxury wool business is . . . *interesting* . . ." the banker's tone was dour, "it presents certain risks we are just not familiar with. However, we do wish you the best of luck."

It was all Deirdre could do not to slam down the phone. This was her third rejection. Her search for new capital was going nowhere. Luxury wool *had* to succeed.

Deirdre returned her attention to the latest financial report from the Count, delivered to her office just yesterday. The farm was still putting far more cash into luxury wool than it was generating. Orders were growing, but it wasn't entirely clear that the new business was on a path to profitability.

For the next hour, Deirdre reviewed the original plan for luxury wool. The business was way behind its projections. But did the plan even have any relevance any longer? They had made so many changes along the way.

Deirdre decided she needed a sounding board. She wanted to talk with someone objective. Someone analytical. Someone like *Einstein.*

No surprise, Deirdre found him in his laboratory, happily absorbed in his research. "I need your advice," she said.

"Of course you do!" the rooster crowed, pushing his microscope aside. He loved it when others recognized his brilliance. Deirdre invited Einstein to join her next meeting with Mav.

At the meeting the following day, Mav gave copies of his order sheet to Deirdre and Einstein, though he couldn't fathom why the odd bird was a part of the meeting. "I get three or four more of these orders from boutique apparel makers every day," Mav explained. "Andrea's strategy of targeting smaller producers seems to be working out very well."

"That's great," Deirdre said. Then she pulled out the plan for luxury wool. "But we also need to talk about how you're doing against your projections."

Mav shifted uncomfortably in his seat. He knew Deirdre had the numbers in front of her. There was no point in trying to hedge.

"Those numbers were based on the best information we had at the time. But you know as well as I do that we were making a lot of guesses. Our initial projections were very optimistic."

"Mav, compared to the other business units, you're not even close to plan," Deirdre responded. "I just reviewed bovine ops. They are within just 2 percent of plan."

Mav took a swig of his energy drink, MusTang. Was it he or was it getting really hot in the room? "Yeah? Well, that's great. But Deirdre, luxury wool has made some big changes since we launched, like manufacturing many more products and taking on a new sales strategy."

"We've already invested more in this business than we anticipated," Deirdre countered. "How much longer until cash flow turns positive?"

Mav really didn't know. He had been incredibly busy focusing on operations, working with his team, visiting customers, perfecting the manufacturing process, and trying to make peace between the sheep and alpaca. He hadn't slept well in as many nights as he could remember. How could he possibly have found time to revise the plan?

"I have a question." Einstein spoke up for the first time. Until now he had seemed absorbed in polishing his thick glasses. "When you two launched this experiment—"

"This is no experiment, Einstein," Deirdre interrupted. "The future of the farm depends on this business."

Einstein looked at Deirdre with a mix of curiosity and exasperation. He silently estimated the difference in their IQs to be forty to fifty points. Perhaps the best tactic was to employ the Socratic method of guided questioning in order to inspire critical thinking.

"Is the luxury wool business *new* to us?" he asked, addressing both Deirdre and Mav.

The two nodded in unison.

"And when we launched, would you say that the outcome was *certain* or *uncertain*?" Einstein continued.

"*Un*certain," said Deirdre.

"Completely uncertain," Mav emphasized.

"Sounds like an experiment to me." Einstein stroked his wattle and grinned. He loved being right all the time.

"Okay, it's an experiment," said Mav. "So what?"

"What was your hypothesis?" Einstein asked.

"Einstein! This is a business, not a geeky search for the perfect genetically enhanced chicken!" Mav was testy.

"Go on," Deirdre instructed Einstein.

"Hypothesis!" Einstein said. "Every experiment starts with a hypothesis. It's a set of assumptions about what you expect to happen. It's really just a *story* about how you expect the business to succeed."

"Well, then we had one," Mav said defensively. "We had a plan. It told the story of how we expected to succeed."

"Did it turn out that your hypothesis was correct?"

"Not exactly," said Mav.

"What do you mean?"

"We've made some changes since then."

"You changed the hypothesis?" asked Einstein.

"If you say so."

This ruffled Einstein's feathers. "Mav, you can't just go around changing your hypothesis whenever you feel like it! That's not *disciplined.* It's just random. How do you expect to *learn* from your experiment?"

Mav sighed. "We're not planning on writing up a lab report, Einstein. We're trying to earn money, not win a Nobel Prize."

Nobel Prize indeed, thought Einstein. Winning that particular honor was his secret ambition. But for now, how was he going to explain the point he was trying to make? The rooster started jumping and flapping his wings, something he always did to help himself think—and in this case, stall for time.

Abruptly, he stopped. "I've got it!" he squawked. "I'm sure you have heard of the First Law of running business experiments." Einstein made sure his tone implied that anyone with half a brain would know what he was talking about, but in truth, he had just invented the First Law.

Mav and Deirdre shook their heads.

"*Learning first, profits second,*" Einstein announced.

Blank stares.

"*Learning first, profits second! Learning first, profits second! Learning first, profits second!*" he squawked.

More blank stares.

"Look," he said, "it just means that **if you put learning *first*—learning through *disciplined experimentation*—you'll make better decisions and you'll actually get to profitability sooner.** Learning *leads* to profits."

Mav could just imagine Bull's reaction to the notion of putting profits second. It wouldn't be pretty. Deirdre, on the other hand, was intrigued. "What are the implications, Einstein? How do we focus, as you say, on learning first?"

"You're asking me how you learn from an experiment?" Einstein realized he actually might have overestimated the intelligence of his audience. He jumped and flapped his wings again, this time for theatrical flair. "One, state a hypothesis. Two, predict what will happen. Three, measure results. Four, assess lessons learned by comparing your predictions to actual outcomes."

Mav rolled his eyes. Deirdre didn't.

"Einstein, you may be on to something," she said. "I'd like you to work with Mav—"

"Say what?" Mav almost spewed his energy drink.

Deirdre ignored the reaction. "Einstein, I'd like you to help Mav figure out what we've learned so far about luxury wool. Help him articulate our current hypothesis. Help him make the best possible estimate of future cash flows."

Einstein roosted in his chair a moment, deciding to play hard to get. "But my lab work—the genetically enhanced—"

"This is more important," Deirdre interrupted, fixing her gaze on the bizarrely intelligent bird. Now was not the time for anyone on the farm to be playing games. "If the luxury wool business doesn't succeed, you may not have the opportunity to genetically enhance anything."

Einstein, for once, was at a loss for words.

Chapter 17

A T THEIR FIRST working session, Einstein handed Mav a blank piece of paper. "We need to write a new business plan from scratch," he stated.

"That just sounds like more work," Mav argued. He looked at the files already stacked on his desk.

"The luxury wool business is too different from the farm's other operations," Einstein explained. "We can't use our standard planning templates."

Together, they put a plan on paper and highlighted all the critical assumptions. Then Einstein made sure Mav had a disciplined process to follow. He urged the stallion to plot every result as a *trend* so he could quickly identify new evidence and lessons learned.

"It's imperative we meet once a month," Einstein emphasized, "to go over the latest numbers, decipher lessons learned, and discuss possible changes in direction."

"Just what I need, more meetings," Mav groaned.

"*Au contraire.*" Einstein loved to occasionally toss in a little French. "I've persuaded Deirdre that you don't need to attend her regular review meetings with the other business unit leaders. While she wasn't convinced at first, my logic won the day, naturally."

"Your logic," Mav repeated, cradling his head between his hooves.

"Luxury wool is an experiment," Einstein reminded Mav. "The other businesses are not experiments. They've been around for years. The conversations are just too different. Deirdre has requested an update from us each time we review the plan. Our meetings will ensure we stay on track."

Another month raced by on the farm. One morning, Mav was in his office going over more numbers when two sharp raps sounded at his door. It was Andrea's signature knock. As usual, the alpaca entered his office without waiting for an invitation.

"It's time to invest in social media websites," she said, never one to waste time with pleasantries like *hello*. "Most of the animals on the farm have never used Farmbook or Tweeter, let alone the newest camelid site, Spitter."

Mav nodded. He'd been hearing a lot about the value of social media.

"I want to hire a new full-time marketing associate," Andrea said, "someone who can devote all her time to marketing luxury wool online."

"Have you been eating some funky grass?" Mav asked, eyes bulging. Hiring someone new would take cash, and cash was in short supply.

"We have to feed our network of friends—those interested in luxury alpaca wool—with new information all the time. Otherwise, they'll lose interest," Andrea pressed her case. "I just don't have the time to be online that much."

Mav knew that Andrea was right in principle. But there simply wasn't any money.

"Mav, if this works, it could take us to the next level in the business. And maximizing social media actually could be a less expensive way to sell our product than anything else we are doing."

Suddenly, the stallion had an inspiration. "Maisie!" he shouted.

"Maisie?" Andrea looked around. "Where?"

But then she caught on and grinned, something Mav

had never seen her do before. "Yes, Maisie!" she said. "Why didn't I think of her myself?"

"Maisie would bring incredible energy to the job," said Mav. "Her passion is exactly what we need online."

Later that evening, he passed the idea by Einstein. Over the past several weeks of collaborating, the horse and the rooster had actually developed some respect for one another. Mav saw the value of following a disciplined process for running experiments, and Einstein showed some curiosity about what it took to be a great business leader.

"It's important to note that making the investment of Maisie's time means a change to our hypothesis," Einstein observed.

"We can't get tied up in too much analysis," Mav responded. "We need to learn as fast as possible."

Mav's words warmed Einstein's heart. The stallion really had been listening to his lectures. "Yes. Absolutely!" Einstein was so excited he shed a few feathers. "You could almost think of this as a separate experiment!"

"What do you mean?"

Einstein paused. Here was another critical concept he needed to explain in terms so clear that even a non-genius could follow. "You know that stuffed animal Thomas always carried with him when he was just a tiny foal?"

"Um, if you say so." Mav had never known Einstein to be sentimental.

"It was a stuffed dog," Einstein continued, "but an unusual one. If you opened a flap in its underside, you could extract six little stuffed puppies."

"My goodness, look at the time," Mav tapped his pocketwatch.

"I'm getting to the point!" Einstein jumped and flapped, something Mav hadn't witnessed since their first meeting in Deirdre's office. "It's the Second Law of running a business experiment!" Einstein announced. He hoped Mav hadn't figured out he was inventing the laws on the fly.

"Inside a big experiment, there are little experiments," he explained.

"So, you are saying that we run this social networking initiative as a distinct experiment?" Mav asked.

"Yes. As *one piece* of the big experiment. We look for evidence that shows it's either working or not working. It is critical that **we gather evidence to validate *each* major expenditure.**"

Mav immediately took the proposal to Deirdre. He shared with her what Einstein had said about validating each major expenditure.

"Mav, are you sure social networking is a good idea?"

"All I can promise is that we'll test it as quickly and cheaply as possible."

Deirdre heard a distant rumbling out her window. When she glanced outside, she saw McGillicuddy parking his enormous tractor at the end of the lane. What was it going to take to get him to back off?

"Do it," she told Mav.

Chapter 18

A FEW WEEKS LATER, Stella couldn't sleep. She saw a light
on in Maisie's stall and dropped in, unannounced.
The cow was hard at work, typing her latest Farmbook
entry.

"*Stellalalala,*" Maisie greeted the sheep warmly.

"Enjoying your new role?" Stella asked.

"It's *farmtastic!*" Maisie gushed, using her new
favorite word. From the minute Mav and Andrea had
offered her the assignment of social media marketing
guru, the cow had given 110 percent. And now her
efforts were paying off. Andrea had even shared data
with Maisie that showed that the awareness of the wonders of alpaca wool was rising, and social networking
was the reason!

"You wouldn't believe how many fashion mavens are
out there in cyberspace," Maisie continued. "I wish I'd
discovered Farmbook a long time ago. I have *so* many
new friends."

Stella smiled, but Maisie could tell something was
wrong. "Why so blue, dear?" she asked.

"I broke up with Alejandro tonight."

"You did what?" Maisie looked flabbergasted. "I'm so sorry. What happened?"

"Alejandro invited me to move to Peru. But I decided I'd just be leaving too much behind. I couldn't give it all up for him."

"There, there," Maisie soothed. "There will be other rams . . . or alpaca. Ah, the modern age," she smiled.

"Thanks, Maisie." Stella wiped away a tear.

"Wait one second, I have something for you."

Maisie rummaged through a pile of clothes in the corner of her stall, emerging with a new hat of her own design. Naturally, it was made of Windsor Farm's alpaca

wool. A bouquet of tulips sprouted from the top. She planted it on Stella's head.

"It's perfect!" Maisie exclaimed. "Wear this hat and you'll be shooing away new suitors every day!"

🐎 🐎 🐎

Four annual performance reviews sat on Deirdre's desk. The ones for the heads of bovine ops, ovine ops, and crops were straightforward and positive. All three managers were within 2 percent of plan. At Windsor Farm, your plan was your promise. Marcus had been adamant about that, and Deirdre was pleased to note that all three of these leaders had delivered what they promised.

And then there was Mav.

Deirdre reread the handwritten note from Bull tucked in Mav's file. *Never seen a miss this bad. Time for someone else to run luxury wool?*

Deirdre grimaced at the suggestion. Maybe Bull was right. Luxury wool was still far from cash-flow positive. In fact, this experiment to save the farm only seemed to be sinking it faster. She understood that a *worse-before-better* trajectory was inevitable for any innovation initiative. But how much *worse* could the farm handle before going under?

Still, she knew Mav had the toughest assignment of all the managers, so it was only fair to evaluate him on different standards. But what standards? No animal at Windsor had ever received a free pass. She summoned Einstein to her office. "Can we have a confidential conversation?" Deirdre asked.

Einstein tweaked his beak as though he were locking it then tossed the imaginary key over his tail feathers.

"I'm working on Mav's performance review," she began. "It's hard. Mav formally revised his plan twice, making his 'promise' a moving target, but even then he missed his plan by a mile. And he's consumed more cash than any of us anticipated. Objectively," Deirdre sighed, "Mav has failed."

"Objectively, you're wrong." The rooster patted his crest, clearly admiring its height.

Deirdre was taken aback. "Einstein, I've always liked your candor. Sort of. Why don't you explain yourself?"

"Who bet the farm on the luxury wool business?"

"I did."

"Who is accountable if the initiative fails?"

"I am."

"What is Mav's job?"

"To deliver!" Deirdre responded without thinking.

"That sounds like something Bull would say," Einstein replied.

"What's wrong with that? Bull does a great job. He's tough as nails and gets results."

"Yes! And the farm needs Bull. But Bull's approach won't work for evaluating innovation leaders."

"So you're saying I *shouldn't* hold Mav accountable?"

"No! Mav must face just as much rigor and discipline as anyone else!" Einstein was growing more and more frustrated. To help him think, he resorted to his usual trick.

"For goodness' sakes!" Deirdre said. "Stop all that jumping and flapping!"

"Deirdre," Einstein couldn't resist one last flap, "have I not yet shared with you the Third Law of running a business experiment?" He knew, of course, that laws should come in threes.

Deirdre reached for the bottle of aspirin in her desk drawer.

"The innovation leader's job is *to execute a disciplined experiment."*

"That's it?"

"That's a lot! If you run a disciplined experiment, you learn quickly. If you learn quickly, you make better decisions. If you make better decisions, you win! Or at least you lose at the lowest possible cost."

"But I like *numbers*! They are so clean! So unambiguous!" Even as the words left her mouth, Deirdre realized that, lately, there wasn't much of anything to like about the farm's numbers. "Can't I hold Mav accountable for results?" The frustration in her voice reminded her of her son Russell, when he couldn't figure out his math homework.

"To some degree," Einstein conceded. "You can hold Mav accountable for the results from any activity, any portion of the experiment that is well understood and predictable. There are *some* aspects of Mav's job that are like that. For example, you can hold him accountable for controlling the costs of alpaca care. It's hardly any different from sheep care. But most every other aspect of what he is doing is unknown to us and uncertain."

"So, explain this to me. Exactly how do you hold someone accountable for executing a disciplined experiment?"

"Excellent question." Einstein strutted over to the whiteboard on Deirdre's wall and wiped away all the notes and figures that were written on it. At the top of the board he wrote, *How to evaluate the performance of an innovation leader,* and launched into yet another lesson.

Two hours later, the rooster was back in his labora-

tory and Deirdre was ready to talk to Mav about his performance review.

"Mav, as we both know, you are way off plan," Deirdre began. Mav instantly broke out in a cold sweat. "But I recognize that I can't evaluate you based *just* on the numbers."

Phew. Mav hoped he hadn't said this aloud. But this was hopeful news, indeed! The farm had always held its leaders accountable for plan. But maybe he would get more wiggle room as an innovation leader. If the luxury wool venture failed, he could use uncertainty as his excuse!

"Mav, I've decided to postpone your review for a few

months," Deirdre continued. "I'm going to be watching you very closely to evaluate how well you run a *disciplined experiment*. I'm going to assess your performance as an *innovation* leader."

"And how do you do that?" Mav asked.

Deirdre smiled at the thought of Einstein's long list of evaluation points on her whiteboard. She started ticking them off.

"I expect you to have a clear hypothesis.

"I expect you to clearly identify the most critical unknowns.

"I expect you to invest a great deal of time and energy in planning, analyzing results, and deciphering lessons learned.

"I expect everyone on your team to understand the plan and every assumption in it. In fact, I am going to do spot-checks to see if everyone can articulate the same assumptions.

"I expect you to react quickly to new information.

"I am going to question you on more of your decisions.

"You need to clearly understand the evidence behind any changes in direction you make.

"I am going to insist on frequent updates to your plan.

"I am going to . . . "

Mav took copious notes as Deirdre went on and on. Clearly, he thought, an innovation leader's job description left very little wiggle room!

Chapter 19

A Few Months Later . . .

I'VE STILL GOT IT! Mav thought, as he pranced out of Deirdre's office. His first months as the head of Windsor Farm's luxury wool business had been rocky, he had to admit, but now the confident Mav was back, feeling better than ever. Deirdre had just given a glowing review of his performance as an innovation leader.

With Einstein's help, he was running luxury wool as a disciplined experiment. He had met every one of Deirdre's long list of expectations. Every investment was showing results that were trending in the right direction, and he and his team were learning at a fast and furious pace. Mav could barely contain himself. In fact, he thought as he grinned a toothy grin, why *should* he contain himself?

As Mav galloped around the farm, trying to burn off some adrenaline, he reflected on how far his team had come in such a short time. In marketing, Andrea's efforts had already created awareness of Windsor's luxury wool among nearly three-fourths of their target customers, and almost all of them had reported a positive impression of the product. In sales, Matt continued to train new hires, and their productivity was rising. Even better, the sales force had succeeded in modestly raising prices and eliminating discounts.

On the social networking front, Maisie was bringing in several unsolicited orders per day, which was quickly reducing the cost-per-sale for luxury wool. And last, but hardly least, Max and Mav has spent many a long night perfecting every detail of the manufacturing process. As a result, they were seeing lower production costs and higher quality!

In the distance, Mav spotted Rambo, Rex, and Rob having lunch together in the pasture. He slowed as he approached them.

"Anyone for a round of poker late tonight?" he called to his buddies.

The three animals turned their backs and trotted away.

Mav's good mood instantly evaporated. Life on the farm, as he had just been reminded, was one long and stressful day after another. Deirdre and Bull were pushing for every penny. The animals were under tremendous pressure, and nobody would give a hoot about his good performance review. The only thing the rest of the farm understood was that luxury wool was *still* consuming more cash than it was bringing in. Clearly, even his friends blamed him for their troubles!

🐎 🐎 🐎

Deirdre had just sent a happy Mav on his way after his positive performance review when a knock sounded on her door. It was the Count, looking like someone had been plucking at his feathers.

"We have to talk," the turkey announced.

Deirdre's heart sank.

"What now?" she asked nervously.

Two hours later, their closed-door meeting finally over, Deirdre knew what had to be done. She wasn't looking forward to asking still more of the animals, but what choice did she have? Deirdre took two aspirins, a few long, cleansing breaths, and called an emergency farm-wide meeting.

🐎 🐎 🐎

Tails swished nervously as the animals gathered in the barnyard. Rambo, Rex, and Rob formed a formidable block, front and center in the crowd. The agitated sheep toward the back huddled so closely they looked like one giant, quivering cotton ball. Maisie and Stella stood amid a group of antsy alpaca. Worry was etched on all the animals' faces.

"What now?" Rob grumbled. "Maybe Deirdre wants to start hiring us out for kiddie birthday parties?"

Rob was upset about the farm's newest cost-saving initiatives. Just last week, he'd been asked to post a sign at the front gate, advertising local hauling. To his mind, this only broadcasted that the farm had fallen on hard times. It was humiliating!

Rex and Rambo felt equally put out. Not only had they been asked to work longer days, but also to reduce spending in key areas, like fertilizer. Everyone seemed to agree that this particular idea really stunk, especially since less fertilizer now could cost the farm in the long run.

As the animals settled around the barnyard, Deirdre took her place behind the podium of stacked hay bales. Bull, Mav, and Einstein gathered behind her on the platform. Their serious expressions spoke to the gravity of this meeting. Mav appeared skittish as he looked out into the crowd.

"Quiet! Quiet, please!" Deirdre addressed the animals. "As you all know," she started, "Windsor Farm has been experiencing serious, even dire cash-flow problems."

Maisie immediately burst into noisy tears, but then clapped a hoof over her mouth. Like so many others, she had been filled with dread for weeks. What was left for Deirdre to say, except that Windsor Farm was kaput? Still, Maisie adjusted her hat and put on a brave face. She may be out of a job; or, worse yet, have to work for that terrible McGillicuddy, but she refused to appear cowed.

"Each and every one of you has shown remarkable courage and ingenuity during this challenging time," Deirdre said. "First, I'd like to thank the Count, who has done a remarkable job of stretching payments to suppliers, collecting early from customers, and extending lines of credit with banks."

The Count, standing on what used to be the chopping block, nodded in acknowledgment, though his expression remained somber.

"But even the Count's efforts have not been quite enough," Deirdre continued. "There are more tough times ahead. We cannot overlook a single opportunity. We must work even harder—"

"*What?*" one of the animals interrupted. "Are you kidding?"

"We can't possibly work any harder!" another shouted.

An alpaca spit and then mumbled, "Excuse me."

"I have an idea," Rob called out, anger in his voice.

"Rob, settle down," Bull said, moving to Deirdre's side.

"Why don't we get rid of all of the alpaca?" Rob continued, despite Bull's admonition. Someone *had* to say the obvious. "That would solve the cash-flow problem in a hoofbeat. We drop thousands per month in salaries, and exit a business that is costing us dearly."

"Yes!" Rambo shouted. "Now you're talking!" Other animals called out in agreement.

"Out with the new. In with the old!"

"Baaaaad alpaca!"

"Moooove over Mav. It's time to be put out to pasture!" Someone tossed an apple in Mav's direction. Deirdre turned to give Mav a reassuring look. Sure enough, the stallion looked spooked enough to run.

Next to Mav, Einstein started flapping his wings. My goodness, the rooster thought, it didn't take a genius—or maybe it did!—to see that tensions at the farm were at an all-time high. This was entirely predictable, of course. Internal strains naturally hit a peak *after* a new business started to show clear signs of success. Growing ventures consume ever more resources.

"Order! Order!" Einstein shouted, flapping his wings even harder. But the agitated crowd only grew more agitated. Something had to be done, the rooster realized, and with that, he *flew* to the podium and perched on top of it.

Jaws dropped. The animals fell into a stunned silence. Who knew Einstein could fly?

"Now that I have your attention," the winded bird paused to catch his breath, "I have something important to say. Something," he pushed up his glasses and puffed out his chest, "that will make you feel a lot better about luxury wool."

Deidre couldn't help but smile at Einstein's theatrics. Who better than Einstein to crow about the new business's positive indicators? The animals crowded closer, eager to hear what the farm's genius bird had to say.

"Building a luxury wool business is a bold experiment," Einstein continued. "And some of you, understandably, want to abandon it." He pointed rather pointedly at Rob. "Yes, we are all under tremendous pressure. And yes, this new venture is still costing Windsor more money than it is generating. But do you know what is even more important than the tight spot the farm finds itself in right now?"

Einstein waited, relishing the fact that all eyes were upon him.

"Where we are heading tomorrow!" he shouted, whipping away the drop cloth from a nearby easel to reveal a chart with an upward-pointing line.

"Behold," Einstein smacked the chart with his wing, "a positive *trend*! Luxury wool is an experiment that has very nearly proven itself."

The rooster went on to explain at great length how he and Mav had tested and resolved all the major uncertainties related to this new business, and how he strongly believed that luxury wool would be generating positive cash flows within just three months.

"My friends," the rooster concluded, "we simply must do everything we can to stay afloat until then." And

with that, Einstein flapped his wings dramatically and flew off in the direction of his laboratory.

As the rooster made his exit, Deirdre surveyed the crowd. Some faces still looked uncertain. Some of the animals were chatting nervously. Deirdre knew that Einstein had made an impression. With his facts and figures, he had appealed to the animals' minds. But now it was up to her to appeal to their hearts.

Deirdre slowly returned to the podium, gathering herself as the animals halted their conversations and gave her their full attention. She thought of the farm's history, and of the immense responsibility that her father, Marcus, had entrusted in her. Then, she began.

"Do you think it was easy?" Deirdre spoke to the unsettled group with a quiet command in her voice. "Do you think it was easy on JP when the Windsors abandoned the farm?" She gave her listeners time to ponder the question.

"Sure, JP was smart," she eventually continued. "Sure, he was confident. But imagine how much courage it took for him to pursue his dream of *Windsor Farm, Proudly Run by the Animals.* The idea was so bold . . . so *inconceivable* . . . neither humans nor animals thought he had any chance of success."

Deirdre could feel the mood shifting in her audience. All eyes were fixed on her; no one doubted Windsor's proud past.

"What we are doing today," she continued, "building a luxury wool business, it is *hard,* no question about it. But it is not *that* hard. Let us never forget that while tight operations have made us great over the past few decades, it was innovation that made us great in the first place. And it is only through innovation that we can *remain* great!"

At this last statement, Maisie, true to form, burst into more loud sobs. This time, however, they were sobs of relief, and she was not alone. Even the Three Little Bulls were blinking back happy tears. If they could just hang in there for three more months! Deirdre caught Stella's eye and mouthed a thank-you. She would never forget that luxury wool was the young sheep's idea.

As the animals in the barnyard began to talk excitedly, Deirdre motioned for Mav to join her at the podium. These past difficult months, Mav had truly proven himself as a leader. It was time he got the public recognition he deserved.

And Bull! She motioned for him to stand beside her as well. *Faster. Stronger. More efficient.* Every animal understood that Windsor Farm never would have survived without him. Deirdre asked the crowd for its attention, intending to pay tribute to these two special coworkers.

"Three cheers for Mav!" One of the animals cried out, before Deirdre had a chance to say a word.

"Here's to Bull!" another shouted.

"Deirdre rocks!" came yet one more voice.

"Hip hip hooray!"

Finally, after all the hoorays and hugs and high fives had subsided, Deirdre closed the meeting with a heartfelt smile and a call to action.

"Now, let's get back to work, shall we?"

Conclusion

Several Months Later . . .

STELLA AND MAISIE headed toward the walkway near the barn, where all the farm animals were gathering for a special occasion. On the way, Maisie pointed out several sheep and alpaca strolling together, enjoying friendly conversations.

"Now that's nice to see," Maisie sighed happily, but then realized how this might upset her friend. "Stella, I could kick myself." The cow twisted her hat by way of apology. "I mean, I know how upset you were about breaking up with Alejandro. . . ."

"It's all good," Stella started to reassure Maisie, but was interrupted by the buzzing of her BlackBerry.

"Hi, Michael," Stella's voice's grew soft. "Sweetie, I'll call you after work." She tucked the phone back into her wool.

"Sweetie?" Maisie could barely contain herself. "Who's Sweetie?"

"Michael works at Chelsea Farms," Stella confided. "I met him at a barn dance a few weeks ago."

"Oooh," Maisie started twisting her hat again, this time with happiness. "Tell me all about him."

"Well, he's charming, witty, tall. . . ."

"Tall?" Maisie repeated.

"Well, not *that* tall!" Stella replied.

Stella and Maisie were still laughing as they joined the other animals waiting on the walkway.

🐎 🐎 🐎

Deirdre motioned McGillicuddy into her office. She said nothing, waiting for her nemesis to speak.

"I know you're in trouble," the old farmer finally opened. "You're down to basically nothing in the bank."

"Go on," Deirdre said.

"I've made you several offers. *Fair* offers." McGillicuddy took off his seed cap and smoothed down the imaginary hair on his bald head. "You shouldn't have refused me. Now you have no choice."

"You're here with another offer?"

He pulled an envelope out of the front pocket of his overalls, just like he had before.

"You want me to open this now?" Deirdre asked.

"That's okay with me," the man replied.

Deirdre scanned the numbers.

"This is much less than before," she said.

"You're not in the same position, not by a long shot."

Deirdre tested her neighbor with silence.

"Listen," McGillicuddy continued, "if you think you can get a better offer. . . ."

"Do *you* think I can get a better offer?" Deirdre shot back.

More silence.

"Well, what do you think of *this* offer?" McGillicuddy finally asked.

Deirdre tapped her hoof in gleeful anticipation. She knew something that McGillicuddy did not. She knew she had just closed a deal for some new land for her rapidly expanding herd of alpaca. She also knew that the farm's luxury wool business was growing explosively. Just a few months ago, it had generated positive cash flow for the first time. The business was going in one direction: *up*! The farm's big gamble had been a big success.

"You *really* want to know what I think?" Deirdre finally asked.

"Yup," said McGillicuddy.

"I think you can *pound sand*!" She grinned. "And now it's time for you to leave Windsor Farm. For good!"

McGillicuddy slammed the barn door on his way out, the envelope holding his measly offer stuffed back in his front pocket. All the farm animals were waiting for him along the walkway. As the farmer walked through the crowd to where his pickup was parked, they sent him off in their inimitable styles.

"*Cluck-cluck!*"

"*Baaaah!*"

"*Neeeeiggh!*"

"*Cock-a-doodle-doo!*" It was Einstein's loudest crow ever.

Just as McGillicuddy reached his truck, Andrea, quite possibly the world's most elegant alpaca, spat on him.

Deirdre took the happy scene in with quiet satisfaction. Windsor was a family farm—*her* family farm. It was run by animals, and it always would be.

Okay, so who really saved the farm?

Study Guide

Questions for Review

Part 1

Chapter 1   What advantages do human-run farms have over animal-run farms like Windsor? Why does Marcus believe the farm needs a new kind of leader?

Chapter 2   How would Bull run Windsor Farm if he were in charge? What offer does Deirdre make to Bull to keep him on the farm?

Chapter 3   What is special about Windsor's history?

Chapter 4   What are the trends in Windsor's finances? When Deirdre discusses the farm's declining performance with Bull and the Three Little Bulls, what do they propose?

Chapter 5   How do Bull and the Three Little Bulls react to Deirdre's Big Idea Hunt?

Chapter 6   What are the positive attributes of Stella's idea, the luxury wool business?

Chapter 7   Why is Bull resistant to the idea of moving quickly into luxury wool? What is Deirdre's opposing point of view? What occurs to Deirdre just after the celebration of the farm's commitment to luxury wool?

Chapter 8   Why do Bull and Deirdre select Mav to run the luxury wool business? Why is Mav excited about taking the job? What is Deirdre's logic for having Mav report to Rambo?

Chapter 9   What are the first few barriers that Mav confronts in his effort to build the luxury wool business? How does Mav respond?

Part 2

Questions for Deeper Reflection

Part 1

Chapter 1   As his last act, Marcus wanted to create change on Windsor Farm. What options other than turning the farm over to Deirdre might he have considered?

Chapter 2   Is Bull part of the problem or part of the solution? What are Deirdre's options with respect to Bull?

Chapter 3   Does Windsor have a history of innovation? How has innovation at Windsor changed over the years?

Chapter 4   How would you characterize the ideas for improvement put forth by Bull and the Three Little Bulls?

Chapter 5   What pressures are Bull and the Three Little Bulls under? How do these pressures explain their reaction to Deirdre's Big Idea Hunt?

Chapter 6   Businesspeople typically put much more energy into a Big Idea Hunt than they put into the effort to turn an idea into something real, like a new product or business. Why do you think this is?

Chapter 7   In your experience, where do the best new ideas come from?

Chapter 8   Is Mav the best choice for running luxury wool? Should Mav accept the job of leading luxury wool? Would you? How can Rambo, Mav's new boss, help ensure the success of luxury wool? Should Bull be emphasizing *We Must Work Harder* at a time like this?

Chapter 9   What are the motivations affecting the characters that create difficulties for Mav? Why couldn't Rambo help?

work it out on their own? What do you think of Deirdre's temporary solution of getting help from Chelsea Farms?

Chapter 16   Why is Deirdre struggling to evaluate the progress of luxury wool? Why do you imagine Mav hasn't been paying much attention to his original plans for the business? Is it only because Mav has so much keeping him busy? Is it possible to manage a new business like a disciplined scientific experiment?

Chapter 17   Mav promises only that he'll test the possibility as quickly and cheaply as possible. Should that be sufficient for Deirdre?

Chapter 18   Has Mav failed? What do you think would happen to Mav at this point if Bull were in charge of the farm?

Chapter 19   Was Einstein the best animal to explain that luxury wool was on a clear trajectory to success? Why? What could Mav have done differently to keep the animals on his side, even during the periods of greatest stress?

Final Questions for Reflection

1. Who saved the farm?
2. What was the most important contribution of each of the main characters: Stella, Marcus, Deirdre, Bull, Mav, Maisie, Rambo, Andrea, Einstein?
3. In the real world, who do you think would get the most credit?
4. If given the opportunity to start over, should Deirdre do anything differently? If so, what specifically?